RED-FOO' in

Amanda Ebenhack

© 2012 by ECO Herpetological Publishing & Distribution.

ISBN 978-0-9767334-4-7

No part of this book may be reproduced or utilized in any form or by any means, electronic or mechanical, including photocopying, recording, or by any information storage or retrieval systems, without permission in writing from the publisher.

Copies available from:

ECO Herpetological Publishing & Distribution
P.O. Box 376, Rodeo ,NM 88056
4 Rattlesnake Canyon Rd, Rodeo, NM 88056
Phone: 575-557-5757
Fax: 575-557-7575

email: ecoorders@hotmail.com
website: http://www.reptileshirts.com

LIVINGART publishing
http://www.livingartpublishing.com

Zoo Book Sales
http://www.zoobooksales.com

Design and layout by Russ Gurley.
Cover design by Chad DeBoard.

Printed in China.

Front cover: An adult Red-footed tortoise. Photo by Amanda Ebenhack.
Back cover: A young Red-footed tortoise. Photo by Bill Love.

Acknowledgements

Thanks to my husband for the many years he has put up with my tortoise adventures and for his continuous support of building my natural outdoor enclosures and bringing my design ideas to life.
A big thank you to Dr. Orlando Diaz for the wonderful work he does with tortoises and for helping me to become a better tortoise keeper and rehabilitator.

Thank you to Eileen Hicks for her excellent proof-reading skills.

Photography

Thanks to Eric Krausse, Bill Love, David Lee / Tortoise Reserve, Michael Mayberry, Russ Gurley, Jake Kirkland, Sam Floyd, Marc Cantos / Turtle Source, Fred Gaal, Pat Ruby, Marty La Prees, Orlando Diaz DVM, Brian Ebenhack, Sitara Monica Perez, Alyse De Vries, Tom Crutchfield, Carl Franklin, Chris Hansen, Keith Begin, Kevin McCurley, Joe Heinen, and Linda Putnam for their wonderful photo contributions.

Thank you to David Lee of the Tortoise Reserve for his input on this manuscript. His passionate work with Red-footed tortoises and most of the world's Asian species has inspired me to be a better conservationist.

I would also like to thank Russ Gurley for his continued encouragement and support and Paula Morris for her editing skills.

Dedication

This book is dedicated to my dearly departed friend and mentor Dr. Barbara Bonner.

Barb Bonner DVM. Photo by Pat Ruby.

INTRODUCTION

The black skin and duller markings of a Brazilian Red-footed tortoise.

History

The Red-footed tortoise (*Chelonoidis carbonaria*) has been a popular tortoise in the herpetological trade for decades. These medium-sized tortoises are hardy, beautiful, and one of the most personable tortoises being kept in captivity today. The Red-footed tortoise is native to South America and is found in nature in Panama, Colombia, Venezuela, Guyana, Suriname, French Guiana, Brazil, Bolivia, Paraguay, and Argentina. Red-footed tortoises have also been found on a few Caribbean islands. It is thought these tortoises were introduced in the 17th century as a convenient food source (Pritchard and Trebbau, 1984).

In the 1970s and 1980s thousands of Redfoots were imported from Guyana, Suriname, and Colombia. Although Red-footed tortoises are protected under Appendix II of the Convention on International Trade

A Yellow-footed tortoise explores its habitat. Photo by Alyse De Vries.

in Endangered Species (C.I.T.E.S.) they are still imported from farms in Venezuela, Brazil, and the Suriname/ Guyana area.

The Yellow-footed tortoise is not as colorful as its cousin the Red-footed tortoise, however they are still quite beautiful. Yellow-footed tortoises are the largest tortoise on the mainland of South America. Yellow-footed tortoises are found in southern Colombia, Ecuador, Peru, Venezuela, Guyana, French Guiana, Brazil, and Bolivia. Unlike the savanna-dwelling Red-footed tortoise, the Yellow-footed tortoises inhabit deep humid rainforest areas. They spend a great deal of time in and around water and in the leaves and undergrowth of moist tropical forests.

Taxonomy

There is now little disagreement that Redfoots and Yellowfoots are members of the genus *Chelonoidis*. According to John Iverson, David Fabius, and others, these tortoises, along with the other South American species, including Chaco tortoises (*C.chilensis*) and even the large Galapagos tortoises are now settled within this genus. It is, however, normal to see Redfoots and Yellowfoots listed under both *Chelonoidis* and *Geochelone*.

Because Redfoots have a fragmented distribution, they are variable in size and coloration according to their origin.

Redfoots range in size from only 8-10 inches (20-25 cm) in total length to very large specimens measuring 18-19 inches (46-51 cm) or more.

Gilson Rivas holding the shell of a very large Red-footed tortoise at the research station Rancho Grande in Estado Aragua in northern Venezuela. Photo by Carl Franklin.

Yellowfoots are overall a bit larger than Redfoots, with some specimens reaching 26-28 inches (66-71 cm), though most will only reach 14-16 inches (35-41 cm).

The Red-footed tortoise was described by Spix in 1824.

Original Description: Spix, J. B. de. 1824. Animalia nova, species novae Testudinum et ranarum quas in itinere per Brasiliam annis 1817-1820 jussu et auspiciis Maximiliana Josephi 2. Leipzig. 24 pp.

Chelonoidis carbonaria

Rhodin, A. J., P. P. van Dijk, and J. Parham. 2008. Turtles of the World: Annotated Checklist of Taxonomy and Synonymy. Chelonian Research Monographs No. 5. IUCN / SSC Tortoise and Freshwater Turtle Specialist Group.

Common Name: Red-footed tortoise, Redfoot tortoise, Red-Legged tortoise, or the Savanna tortoise.
Kingdom: Animalia
Phylum: Chordata
Class: Reptillia
Order: Testudines
Family: Testudinidae
Genus: Chelonoidis
Species: carbonaria

The Yellow-footed tortoise was recognized as an individual species by Linnaeus, in 1766.

Original Description: Linnaeus, C. 1766. Systema Naturae, 12th ed. Halae Magdeborgicae. 1: 1-532.

Chelonoidis denticulata

Rhodin, A. J., P. P. van Dijk, and J. Parham. 2008. Turtles of the World: Annotated Checklist of Taxonomy and Synonymy. Chelonian Research Monographs No. 5. IUCN / SSC Tortoise and Freshwater Turtle Specialist Group.

Yellow-footed tortoises (*Geochelone denticulata*) are closely related to the Red-footed tortoise (*Geochelone carbonaria*) as the name suggests. Yellow-footed tortoises generally have yellow scales on their forelegs while Red-footed tortoises generally have red scales on theirs. This however, should not be the sole characteristic to distinguish the two from each other. There are brightly colored Yellowfoots while some Redfoots have muted colorations on the legs. Also some Red-footed tortoises have yellow leg scales.

While there are many differences between the Red-footed and Yellow-footed tortoise, their coloration is the most variable.

Kingdom: Animalia
Phylum: Chordata
Class: Reptillia
Order: Testudines
Family: Testudinidae
Genus: Chelonoidis
Species: denticulata

Tortoises have been around for over 250 million years! These fascinating creatures are worthy of our respect and receiving the best care possible when being kept in captivity.

A very large Amazon Basin Yellow-footed tortoise. Photo by Tom Crutchfield.

Before making the long-term commitment of tortoise ownership please consider their precise needs and your ability to accommodate those needs. The needs of any turtle or tortoise in captivity are based on the conditions in which they live in nature. As tortoise keepers we are responsible for providing those needs to the best of our ability.

Enclosures, whether indoor or outdoor, all have specific elements that offer security, a proper substrate, proper lighting or shade, and a clean accessible water source.

When possible, tortoises benefit greatly from being housed outdoors, especially in the summer months. It is not a happy life for a tortoise

A beautiful adult Red-footed tortoise.

of any size to live out its life in a tub or a tank. Like us, tortoises need the stimulation that comes from exploring a spacious and interesting environment.

This book will show you how to properly care for your Red-footed or Yellow-footed tortoise by replicating as closely as possible their natural environment. By exploring attractive enclosure ideas, planning a correct and varied diet, and offering hydration and health tips, we will help you to keep your tortoise healthy and happy for years to come.

Chapter ONE: Red-footed Tortoises in Nature

A beautiful Red-footed tortoise from the population transplanted to Barbados in the mid 1800s. Photo by Orlando Diaz DVM.

The Red-footed tortoise (*Chelonoidis carbonaria*) is a fascinating tortoise native to South America. The Red-footed tortoise is found in diverse habitats across its range. It can be found in dry grasslands, forest areas, and more humid tropical forest habitats.

The Red-footed tortoise's range includes Panama, Colombia, Venezuela, Guyana, Suriname, French Guiana, Brazil, Bolivia, Paraguay, and Argentina. Red-footed tortoises have also been found on a few Caribbean Islands. It is thought that these tortoises were introduced to the islands in the 17th century as a convenient food source for sailors and settlers (Pritchard and Trebbau, 1984). There is some debate how they arrived on these islands. Some believe the Arawak and Carib Indians may have introduced the tortoises to several islands as a food source (Lescure, 1983; Censky 1988). Watters (1989) believes the tortoises were transferred by the Europeans. Because island tortoise populations are only a few decades old, some

The natural range of *Chelonoidis carbonaria*, the Red-footed tortoise.

believe that they may have derived from escaped or released pets (Vinke and Vinke, 2008). Other authors assume tortoises in the Carribean arrived on their own by crossing the sea on clumps of vegetation they climbed onto during flooding (Lazell 1993; Thomas, 1999).

The Red-footed tortoise is considered a food source in much of its range. Sadly, tortoises, including Red-footed and Yellow-footed

The bodies of Yellow-footed tortoises and a variety of aquatic turtles for sale in a market in Peru. Photos by Michael Mayberry.

tortoises, are considered "fish" by the Catholic church and during holy week Redfoots and Yellowfoots are consumed in huge numbers in South America. They are captured and shipped throughout South America to be sold and butchered in local markets. Turtles and tortoises can tolerate long periods of time without food and water and can be stored alive, without refrigeration in areas where it is very hot and where there is no electricity.

Climate

The changes from the wet season to the dry season are probably the most important aspects in the day-to-day lives of Red-footed tortoises.

Red-footed tortoises living in northern South America from Colombia, Venezuela, and east to northern Brazil, and those living in the Bolivian Amazon lowlands experience wetter tropical conditions than the Red-footed tortoises living in the Bolivian and Argentinean Gran Chaco, southern Brazil, and Paraguay. Here the Redfoots live in arid subtropical conditions (Vinke and Vetter, 2008).

The seasons in South America are the opposite of those in the United States. Our winter is their summer and their winter is our summer.

The misty tropical forest habitat of Brazilian Red-footed tortoises.

This is an important consideration when purchasing an imported tortoise. South America's weather varies from north to south. The northeastern area is the hottest on the continent where summer temperatures exceed 100° F (38° C).

On the savanna. Red-footed tortoise habitat near Cerro Pelon, Venezuela. Photo courtesy of Quetzal Dwyer and Sitara Monica Perez.

Redfoots habitat in the Amazon River basin is hot and humid throughout the year with an average temperature of 81° F (27° C). The inland plateaus have a mild climate while the coastal habitat of the east and southeast are much warmer.

Rainfall

The heaviest rainfall in South America occurs in the upper Amazon with a yearly average of 115 inches (292 cm). In some places this is even higher.

Diet in Nature

Red-footed tortoises are omnivorous. In the wild, they graze on green leafy plants, flowers, fallen fruits, invertebrates, and occasionally carrion.

Moskovits and Bjorndal (1990) noted that in addition to flowers, leaves, and fruits, Redfoots and Yellowfoots ate carrion (including Agouti, peccary, birds, snakes, lizards, and even deer carcasses). Live prey includes snails, ants, termites, bees, beetles, and butterflies. David Lee of the Tortoise Reserve reports seeing an adult Red-footed tortoise chase down and eat a live snake. An amazing story related to me by tortoise breeder, Doug Beard, is of a friend of his who heard an awful commotion in the underbrush while in the field in Bolivia. Expecting a large mammal to break through, instead came crashing through the underbrush a large adult Red-footed tortoise, dragging a dead monkey with two or three other large Redfoots in hot pursuit, trying to take this prize meal away from the noise maker. Other items found in the digestive systems of these tortoises have included mushrooms, sand, soil, pebbles, tortoise feces, and bark.

Other studies, including Castaño and Lugo (1981) reported a preference in *C. carbonaria* for red and yellow flowers. Pritchard and Trebbau (1984) confirmed this by observing Red-footed tortoises in Venezuela. Fruits remain the main component in the diet of this species, comprising up to 70% of the total intake during the wet season and approximately 40% during the dry season. Fruits are normally consumed in a very ripe state after they have fallen from the trees. After fruits, flowers are the second most popular food items. During the dry season, flowers constitute up to about 25% of the diet of this species. The rest of the diet (about 20%) is comprised of green leaves and stems and (about 20%) miscellaneous fungi, mosses, termites, and carrion.

Importation

Red-footed tortoises are still imported from farms in Venezuela and Brazil and tortoises that are taken from the wild are imported from the Guyana/Suriname area. Venezuela, Guyana, Suriname, and Brazil are still exporting tortoises. Only Guyana and Suriname continue to export wild-caught Red-footed and Yellow-footed tortoises. Between the year 2000-2005, an estimated 35,565 Red-footed tortoises and 6,526 Yellow-footed tortoises were exported from South America (Vinke and Vetter, 2008).

Red-footed tortoises in a captive breeding facility in Puerto Mirando, Venezuela. Photo by David Lee / Tortoise Reserve.

Importers that receive tortoises designated for the pet trade place "orders" to the farms and the C.I.T.E.S. office will issue a permit for a certain number of tortoises. There is a quota for how many can be gathered and exported in a certain time period.

Chapter TWO: Anatomy

Red-footed tortoises representing five different "races". Guyana (left), Colombia (middle), and Cherry heads from Paraguay (top) and Argentina (far right). Photo by Bill Love.

Though they are quite variable in size, shape, and coloration across their large range, Red-footed tortoises are one of the most colorful tortoises.

The Shell

The skin and top shell (carapace) is dark brown to black with a stunning contrast of lighter yellow patches, or areolae.

The bottom shell (plastron) is typically a creamy yellowish or tan. A Redfoot's head can have patches of red, yellow, or orange. Redfoots get their name from the large red scales on their forelegs. Redfoots are sometimes called Savanna tortoises or Red-legged tortoises. Considered a medium-sized tortoise, most Redfoots reach a maximum size of 14 inches (36 cm) however some individuals can reach much larger sizes.

Male Red-footed tortoises are larger than females and have concave plastrons. This concavity lets the male more easily mount the female

The head scalation of a beautiful Red-footed tortoise.

during copulation. The curve of the female's carapace, will fit into the concave area of the male's plastron. In most populations of Redfoots, males and females develop an hour-glass figure though this characteristic is more developed in males.

The Head

The Red-footed tortoise's head is triangular when viewed from above. There is a large rounded frontal scale covering the forehead. The large nasal scale in the front above the nose can be partially or completely divided. Smaller scales cover the back of the head and around the eyes. The head is longer than it is wide. A Redfoot's head can sport red, yellow, orange, or any combination of the three.

The Limbs

Redfoots get their name from the large red scales on the forelegs. The front limbs of the Red-footed tortoise are slightly flattened. The front legs are sometimes used to protect the face when they encounter predators. A shy tortoise may pull its head in and cover its face

Leg scales of an adult Red-footed tortoise - front legs (above) and back foot (below).

with its limbs. The limbs are covered with large rounded scales, some of which are overlapping. The back feet are elephant-like without the raised scales so prominent on the front limbs. The front feet of a Red-footed tortoise have five claws while the back feet only have four. There are small scales on the front and back feet continuing to the very bottom of the feet.

The Tail

The tail ranges from gray to black and is decorated with flat, colorful scales.

Plastron view of the tail of the male Red-footed tortoise. Note the larger tail, wider anal notch, and concave plastron of the male.

Plastron view of the tail of the female Red-footed tortoise. Note the shorter tail and angular anal notch.

The tail of a male Red-footed tortoise is considerably longer and thicker than that of the female. When picked up, the male's tail is positioned to one side of the tortoise rather than projecting straight out. His anal notch is wide and oval and the anal notch of the female is wide and angular to allow for passage of the eggs. The female's tail is shorter.

Coloration

Color variations in Redfoots can be subtle or intense. They range from the beautiful Cherry heads of Argentina to the subtly colored yellow Redfoots of Colombia.

An unusual yellow and black Red-footed tortoise from Colombia. Photo by Chris Hansen.

Further compounding the already difficult task of identifying colors and patterns of Redfoots from different regions is the lack of information as to where most tortoises are imported from. For instance, tortoises may not be exported from the actual country in which they were gathered. There are probably even more variations than are currently known. A tortoise farmer in Colombia swears he has three different coloration and patterns from within his region (Lucas, M., pers. com.). This has not been verified in documented photography, however it does reiterate the fact that much more investigation is needed.

Shell Abnormalities

Pyramiding

Pyramiding is when carapace scutes grow vertically (like a pyramid) rather than horizontally. The appearance of the shell looks "bumpy".

A Red-footed tortoise with a minor case of pyramiding.

This condition can be caused by a variety of factors but we know that a lack of environmental humidity in captivity is the primary cause. A diet too high in protein and too low in calcium may be a contributing factor. This is one reason it is so important to maintain the proper levels of humidity while hatchling tortoises are growing. Other factors contributing to pyramiding are not enough fiber, lack of Vitamin D, being kept too cool, or even lack of exercise. While tortoises that are pyramided may never regain a totally smooth shell, new growth will visually appear flat once the husbandry issues are corrected (Fife, 2006).

Irregular Scutes

Occasionally tortoises are seen with irregular scutes. This may consist of an extra scute or a split scute. While this condition occurs in nature, it is most commonly the result of artificial incubation with temperatures that are high. The higher temperatures that cause the split scutes may also produce female hatchlings due to Temperature Dependent Sexual Determination (TDSD) as females are typically produced at higher incubation temperatures.

Chapter THREE: Choosing a Tortoise

A shy, but healthy, young Red-footed tortoise.

In the 1970s and 1980s, thousands of Red-footed tortoises were imported from Guyana, Suriname, and Colombia. Although Red-footed tortoises are protected under Appendix II of the Convention on International Trade in Endangered Species (C.I.T.E.S.), they are still imported from farms in Venezuela, Brazil, and the Suriname/Guyana area. I of course recommend that anyone wanting a Red-footed tortoise for a new pet should search for and purchase a captive-hatched Redfoot. These captive-produced tortoises will be less stressed, are less likely to harbor dangerous internal parasites, and they promote the work of tortoise breeders across the country.

Wild-caught Red-footed and Yellow-footed Tortoises

Red-footed tortoises and Yellow-footed tortoises are hunted for food. They are often kept for long periods of time without food or water until they are slaughtered or shipped off to the pet trade. It is not advisable to start out with a wild-caught Redfoot or Yellowfoot for a

Two young Red-footed tortoises, both produced from parents with pure Colombian stock, showing the variety of specimens within an area. Photo by Bill Love.

pet. This has proven to be quite a challenge even with the most experienced keepers. Tortoises captured for the pet trade are often not given the best of care before importation. Recently imported tortoises often arrive dehydrated, anorexic, stressed, and heavily loaded with parasites. Complicating matters is the fact that they are not likely to immediately acclimate to their new surroundings especially if being kept indoors. Some wild-caught specimens may never adapt to life in captivity.

Never mix a wild-caught tortoise with tortoises you already have. They will need a quarantine period of at least 90-120 days. Soak them in tepid water each day to make sure they are hydrated properly. Wild-caught tortoises should be checked by a veterinarian for parasites and other medical issues.

The Yellow-footed and Red-footed tortoises will benefit from captive-breeding to reduce pressure on wild populations. Once abundant in their native land, their numbers are dwindling due to frequent capture. Tortoises are easily caught by hunters who sometimes use dogs to find them hiding in vegetation. Dry season vegetation is also burned to aide in capture. Some are sold as pets and many others are eaten. Further complicating the situation are the years it takes for a Red-footed tortoise and a Yellow-footed tortoise to reach sexual maturity.

Preparing for a New Family Member

It's best to have your new tortoise's enclosure ready for it before you bring it home. This will avoid stress on everyone. If you have other pets in the home you must consider safety issues for your tortoise.

Dogs and tortoises do not mix! Even the sweetest of dogs that has never hurt a fly will usually instinctively chew on a tortoise. It's your responsibility to keep them safe! Be sure your tortoise's enclosure is secure and away from any pets. Keeping them out of harm's way will help avoid any costly veterinary bills down the road.

Supply Check List

___ Enclosure appropriate for the size of your new tortoise (see Indoor Enclosures) for help with this decision.

___ Substrate that holds humidity
___ Light fixtures (can be purchased at home supply stores). You will need a basking lamp fixture and a strip-light fixture if housing indoors.
___ Proper lamps (one for heat and one for UVB emission)
___ Hide area
___ Shallow water bowl
___ Decorations
___ Calcium, calcium with Vitamin D3, and mineral supplements
___ The phone number of a qualified reptile veterinarian (check www.arav.org to find a reptile veterinarian in your area).

Things to Consider Before Acquiring a Tortoise

Before making the decision that a tortoise is the right pet for you, several factors must be taken into consideration. Please remember tortoises are more of a "watch me" pet. They do not enjoy cuddling in the bed with you, sitting in your lap, or fetching sticks. You must consider the needs of the tortoise and your ability to house, feed, and care for it properly. Tortoises live much longer than most pets. You will have to plan for their future even after you are gone as they can

Tortoise breeder Linda Putnam created this outdoor Red-footed tortoise enclosure with landscape timbers. Photo by Russ Gurley.

live over 40 years. If you feel you can keep a tortoise in the right way, including the ability to pay any unforeseen medical bills, you are on the right track.

Choosing a Species of Tortoise

When choosing a species of tortoise as an addition to your family you will also need to consider several factors. Does your climate allow for the tortoise to spend most of its time outdoors? This might not be possible if you live in an apartment.

People living in hot and dry areas may consider a species that would do better in that environment. Individuals living in cold northern states may consider obtaining a smaller species that is easier to house when being kept indoors the majority of the year.

Red-footed and Yellow-footed tortoises do wonderfully in the humid southeastern United States. However, African Spurred Tortoises and Leopard tortoises do much better in the more arid southwestern United States.

If you decide on a South American tortoise, your next consideration is choosing between a Red-footed or a Yellow-footed tortoise.

When choosing between a Red-footed or a Yellow-footed tortoise, it is helpful to know as much as you can about each species. While their care is almost identical, Yellow-footed tortoises are not quite as hardy, need more shade, and more stable temperatures. They also eat a bit more fruit than Red-footed tortoises. Yellowfoots also spend more time in the water. Red-footed tortoises may be more personable and they stay a bit smaller.

Where to Buy Tortoises

Perhaps one of the most important considerations in acquiring a tortoise is where to purchase them.

Tortoises can be purchased from breeders, specialty pet stores, expos, and reptile shows, and even the internet. In some cases tortoises can be adopted from rescue organizations.

Pet Stores - Large Chain

More and more tortoises are being offered for sale in pet stores. The benefit in purchasing a tortoise from a pet store is you can physically examine the tortoise. Many employees in the larger pet chains are not as knowledgable about these specialized pets. It will be important for you to do your homework to make sure you pick out a healthy tortoise.

Specialty Pet Stores

Specialty pet stores usually have a much larger variety of tortoises for sale. In some cases they may breed their own or at least be able to answer questions about age, what the tortoise has been through, what it is eating, etc. There are some very good specialty reptile stores that have a wonderful reputation and dozens of repeat customers.

At times breeders may sell their hatchlings to specialty pet shops. Ask questions to find out as much as you can about where the tortoise came from. In some cases, tortoises may be imported from breeding farms in South America. While this is not a choice as positive as buying captive-hatched animals, these farms still take pressure off of the wild populations.

Reptile Shows and Reptile Expos

In recent years, reptile shows and expos have become quite popular. Some of these expos are attended by breeders from around the United States. Prices are often competitive and choices are abundant. I would suggest that you don't buy the first tortoise you see. Walk around and visit with some of the vendors. Some may have larger, well-started tortoises instead of small hatchlings. If the tortoises still have their caruncles, or egg teeth, that means they are quite young. Ask lots of questions.

Another good part of expos and shows is they generally have vendors that sell supplies too. In addition, many breeders proudly display tortoises they have hatched themselves.

Breeders that claim to know the sex of a hatchling are pulling your leg. It may be necessary to find a more truthful breeder, as the sexing of hatchlings is nearly impossible, though hatchlings with odd

Tortoise breeders such as Richard Fife and Jerry Fife (pictured with Jerry's daughter Dani) are often displaying at reptile shows and expos. Questions about captive care, housing, and parentage can be answered.

A beautiful, well-planted Red-footed tortoise enclosure in Florida. Photo by Erich Krausse.

or irregular scutes invariably turn out to be females. (Irregular scutes are usually the result of higher incubation temperatures which also produces a higher number of female tortoises.)

Breeders

Breeders are one of the best sources for tortoises. After all they keep their adults healthy enough to breed. Breeders will be able to give you the exact age of the tortoise you are considering purchasing. They also may be able to give you other tips or suggestions pertaining to their care. Another advantage is the tortoise will not have to be shipped which can be stressful.

The Internet

There are websites that allow dealers, breeders, and private individuals to sell their tortoises to the public. Often there is no health guarantee as once the tortoise is in your hands the seller cannot be responsible for poor husbandry that leads to an early demise. Some Internet sellers will guarantee live arrival and maybe a week health guarantee but that's usually as far as it goes. Some disadvantages of buying tortoises over the Internet is the mystery of where they came from. Some tortoises may have been shipped several times before being offered to you. This can be very stressful to them. Another disadvantage is the inability to choose your tortoise and examine it for potential health issues.

Choosing your tortoise is very important as it will be with you for many years. Investigate the sources you are considering buying from. Some breeders do sell on the Internet. There are well-known breeders who have been around for a long time. They have a good reputation for producing healthy active tortoises. If you decide to buy a tortoise from the Internet, make sure it is from a reputable source. Often individual pictures of tortoises will be offered to make choosing easier.

Do not believe everything you read! Some people will say anything to get you to buy from them. There may be claims of a tortoise being captive-hatched, being a long-term captive, being a proven breeder, or even some new color morph the seller has made up while typing the ad.

Do not trust these sellers unless you know them or can verify their reputation.

Tortoise Rescues

There are turtle and tortoise rescues throughout the United States that offer tortoises including Redfoots for adoption. In some cases a tortoise keeper's life situation has changed, leaving them unable to care for their tortoises. Adopting a tortoise has several benefits - the obvious being offering a home to a tortoise in need.

Choosing a specific tortoise.

Ideally, being able to physically see and hold the tortoise you are considering purchasing is best. One good indicator of health can be found by examining the enclosure in which the tortoise is currently in. The enclosure should be clean and spacious. The water bowl should be clean and full. Make sure the Redfoots or Yellowfoots are not mixed with other species. It is not recommended to mix tortoises from different parts of the world. If this condition exists you should not buy them.

Once you find a tortoise you are interested in, you should check it for the following:

The tortoise should be heavy for his size, alert, and active.
The tortoise should have strong limbs and push off of your finger with force.
The shell should be hard and uniform, free of any bumps or irregularities to the scutes.
The eyes should be alert and clear and free of any discharge.
The nares (nostrils) should be open and clear and free from discharge.
The vent should be clean and free from any redness or bumps.
The mouth should be free from lumps, injuries, or discharge.
The tortoise should walk high on its legs, with the shell off the ground and its head out.

Bringing Your Tortoise Home

There is some degree of stress to the tortoise whether bringing it home from a breeder or reptile show and especially if it is shipped.

Having the tortoise's new home set up and ready will eliminate some of this stress. It may take a day or two for your tortoise to adjust to its new surroundings. Don't worry if it hides or refuses to eat for a few days. Once the tortoise feels secure, normal activities such as eating and wandering around the enclosure will resume.

Quarantine

If you have an existing tortoise, and are aquiring a new one, you will need to quarantine it. This is particualirly important when introducing an adult tortoise to one already in your collection. If you have no idea where they came from, there is a possibility the tortoise could be wild-caught. While wild-caught tortoises may be cheaper to purchase in the long run they will be more expensive. Wild-caught tortoises endure large amounts of stress which produces in them a

This wide-eyed Cherry head Red-footed tortoise is not only beautiful but healthy and alert. Photo by Marc Cantos.

compromised immune system. Living conditons that are cramped or dirty can cause a proliferation of parasites. Even if the tortoise looks and acts fine it could transfer illness to your tortoises. A 90 day quarantine period is recommended if the tortoise is suspected of being wild-caught. Catching tortoises in nature for the pet trade also puts pressure on wild populations that are already in trouble.

Chapter FOUR: Hatchling Care

A young tortoise should be surprisingly heavy, active, and alert.

If you have made the wise decision to start out with a captive-bred Red or Yellow-footed tortoise, you have the opportunity to raise them correctly. The goals you should have as a keeper are to offer proper husbandry including an enclosure and a diet that will allow for smooth, even growth.

Hatchling tortoises will spend much of their time hiding. It is important to offer them security. A hide log placed in the dark side of their enclosure will offer a safe, moist place to hide.

A shallow water dish should be available at all times.

A basking area should be provided with a heat lamp. This light should be placed over the opposite end of their hiding area. You will want to adjust the lamp's bulb strength or height until their basking area is in the 80-82° F (27-28° C) range.

Young Cherry head Red-footed tortoises eating a salad.

Feeding Hatchlings

The diet of hatchling Red-footed tortoises is very similar to that of the adults. However, we don't generally offer fruit until they are about six months old. It is very beneficial to introduce them to natural foods such as grasses, dandelions, Hibiscus, and non-toxic weeds at a young age. The recognition of these plants as foods will encourage natural grazing behavior when they are old enough to be housed outdoors.

Hatchling Redfoots may not eat until around a week after hatching because they are still living off of the nutrients in their yolk sacs. In about a week start offering nutritious greens such as "Spring Mix", greenleaf, redleaf and romaine lettuce, mustard greens, dandelions, and flowers. As they grow, their appetites will increase and the salads you offer can become more diverse.

Don't expect your baby Redfoot to come running to you just yet. Hatchlings are often very shy and will spend a great deal of time just hiding. They will spend time in a pile of moist sphagnum moss or

Similar to observations made with adult Red-footed tortoises, hatchlings (if housing several together) may choose to crowd into a single hiding place, even if given many suitable shelters. Photo by Joe Heinen.

under the shelter that you have provided for them. In time they will see you as the food provider and gradually become friendlier. Start by offering them a small piece of banana or strawberry as a treat and soon they will come running for these treats.

Observed Hatchling Behavior

I have observed hatchling tortoises completely burying themselves in moist substrate. This behavior is similar to North American box turtles and some species of Asian box turtles of the genus *Cuora*. The young tortoises wedge themselves under the substrate, exposing only a small portion of their heads.

This is yet another reason to have the proper moist substrate that allows hiding. Moisture from the substrate will absorb through their skin, keeping it hydrated and healthy.

Failure to Thrive in Hatchlings

In the wild 50-80% of hatchlings never reach adult breeding size. This is mostly due to predation. Many animals eat the young tortoises and the eggs of Red-footed tortoises. These predators include South America's Giant armadillos, tegus, snakes, and birds.

A condition called Failure to Thrive may occur in some hatchlings produced in captivity. One symptom may be a hatchling not growing, especially in comparison to other siblings. The tortoise may have a soft shell or softening of the shell that was once hard. Even if all conditions of good husbandry are addressed, the tortoise may eat, may be active, and simply not grow or "thrive". There is no known cure for this condition. Hatchlings with Failure to Thrive syndrome will eventually manifest symptoms such as respiratory issues, sunken eyes, and lethargy before they die. Refer to Choosing a Tortoise in Chapter THREE to decrease the chances you choose a tortoise with this condition.

Moisture is very important as hatchlings can dehydrate very easily. The preferred substrate for a hatchling Redfoot is moistened long fiber sphagnum moss. Rinse the moss well and squeeze out excess water. Babies will spend a great deal of time hiding. It is important to offer them security. A hide log, full of damp moss, placed in the dark side of their enclosure will offer a safe, moist place to hide.

A water dish that is easily accessible should be available at all times. Hatchlings should be soaked twice

A simple enclosure for Red-footed tortoise hatchlings.

When they are soaked in a shallow dish of tepid water, Red-footed tortoise hatchlings often defecate.

a week for about 10 minutes. Misting them as they sit in the soaking dish will encourage drinking as well as elimination. This will help keep their enclosure cleaner.

Chapter FIVE: Indoor Enclosures

A large indoor enclosure that provides both warmth and humidity. Photo by Keith Begin.

Tortoises should be permitted to live outdoors whenever possible however it may be necessary to house them indoors during inclement weather or while hatchlings grow. There are many considerations that need to be addressed in properly housing tortoises indoors. These include the type of enclosure, the size of the enclosure, substrate, lighting, water source, and hide area(s). All of these elements are very important in giving your tortoise the best care possible.

Glass Terrariums

A common misconception is that glass tanks make good enclosures for tortoises because they can see through them. Tortoises have no concept of glass and may try to climb through it. If your tortoise appears stressed in a glass terrarium, a good idea is to tape colored paper or some other visual barrier 4-6 inches around the bottom of the tank. This will block their view. In some cases, terrariums may hold the humidity better, especially if the enclosure is within an air-conditioned environment. Choose an enclosure that is longer than it is tall to allow plenty of room for exercise.

Small Tortoises

Always choose the largest enclosure possible for your available space. The most important aspect of choosing your enclosures is the ability to provide a temperature gradient within the enclosure. Your tortoise needs the ability to warm up when they are cold and cool off when they are too hot. This cannot be achieved in an enclosure that is too small. The enclosure should be at least (30"l x 12"w x 12"h) There are a variety of polyethylene and plastic tubs on the market. These tubs work well as tortoise enclosures as they are relatively lightweight and easy to clean.

Cement mixing tubs, Rubbermaid tubs, and sweater boxes are all good choices for a small Red-footed tortoise.

As your tortoise grows so should its enclosure.

When the time has come to upgrade your tortoise's living area there are many retailers and specialty pet stores that sell tubs specially made for tortoises. A medium tortoise's enclosure should be no smaller than (48"l x 13"w x 16"h). Again, this is to provide a proper temperature gradient. Tubs that are 72"l x 36"w x 12"h are distributed by some pet stores and herp supply retailers. Vision and Waterlandtubs make great light-weight tubs that are easy to clean and move. These tubs make excellent enclosures for small to medium tortoises.

Stock tanks made of galvanized metal or plastic also make roomy enclosures. These can be found at most farm supply stores. Though they may be heavier, they are also very sturdy.

Wooden Enclosures and Tortoise Tables

If you're creative with a hammer and nails, a wooden enclosure can be custom made to fit your desired space. Be sure to seal the wood with polyurethane. Let the fumes dissipate for several days before introducing your tortoise to its new home. Treating the wood with a protective seal will help keep the moisture Redfoots need from warping the wood.

Tortoise Tables

Tortoise tables are like other wooden enclosures however they usually are made right on a table. Tortoise Tables are enclosures and stands together. Some keepers attach wheels so the tables can be rolled outside for access to natural sunlight. Tortoise Tables can have more than one level with multiple enclosures for efficient use of space. Some keepers sink cat litter pans or other small tubs into the bottom of the table to add a water source or fill the pans with moss to provide a humid hide area. Non-toxic plants can be added inside for grazing and stimulation.

Lighting and Heat

Lighting is another debatable subject as most baby tortoises of any species spend a great deal of time hiding in the darkest area of their habitat. A warm ambient temperature in the room the tortoise enclosure resides in is a good choice. However, this is not always possible. If a warm (80 to 82° F) ambient temperature cannot be provided then an area that reaches 85° F (27° C) should be provided by placing a basking lamp in one corner of their enclosure. Clamp lamps work well. The basking area should be at the opposite end from their hiding area.

Whenever possible heating sources should be run through a thermostat. Red-footed tortoises do not enjoy powerful lighting such as mercury vapor bulbs. Though they emit lots of heat and UVB rays, these powerful bulbs can be dangerous to a delicate hatchling's eyes.

A ceramic heat emitter bulb can be used as well. After the first year has passed they are much more tolerant of the mercury vapor bulbs. A full-spectrum fluorescent light is necessary to provide UVB for Vitamin D syntheses. These are the tube lights. The light should be placed at least 12 inches (31 cm) above the enclosure's floor.

Tortoises not exposed to natural sunlight or UVB run a risk of developing Metabolic Bone Disease (MBD), a dangerous condition that occurs commonly in young tortoises that are growing quickly and in egg-laying females. This condition causes tortoises to have soft shells and growth deformities. MBD is life-threatening. Experts agree that MBD is the most common cause of death in many types of young, captive reptiles (Highfield, 2002).

The author's hatchling enclosure.

UVB-emitting lamps should not be obstructed by glass, plastic, or even mesh. These can significantly (or completely) block the rays beneficial for your captive reptile. The output of the lamps should be tested regularly and when UVB output gets low, they should be replaced.

Substrate

Substrate choices are one of the most critical factors in raising healthy tortoises. Baby Redfoots love to snuggle down in the soft sphagnum moss. A long-fibered sphagnum moss is soft and holds humidity. It's imperative to keep Redfoot hatchlings from dehydrating. An enclosure that is dry can cause pyramiding and eye problems as dusty substrates can irritate the eyes. Breathing in dust can cause respiratory problems as well. Tortoises have the ability to absorb moisture through their skin. Having the correct substrate and humidity will give your tortoise's skin a healthy appearance. Many husbandry problems can be linked back to improper substrate.

Note: Keep a misting bottle near the enclosure to spray the substrate as needed to maintain the proper humidity.

The best choices for substrate are:

Long-fibered sphagnum moss
1/2 Peat moss and 1/2 organic top soil mixture
1/3 Peat moss, 1/3 play sand, and 1/3 sphagnum moss mixture
Mulch that is free of dyes (for tortoises that are subadult and older)

Poor choices for substrate are:

Walnut shells / cracked corn (risk of impaction if swallowed
Sand (risk of impaction)
Rabbit pellets (molds easily, dusty, does not hold humidity)
Reptile carpet (catches nails, does not hold humidity)
Pine and cedar shavings (emits toxic oils)

A large indoor enclosure that provides both warmth and humidity. Photo by Keith Begin.

Humidity

It may be difficult to keep the humidity up in your tortoise's enclosure. This is especially true in very warm states where air conditioning is in use. There are several remedies for this situation. A humidifier may be added in the room in which the enclosure is located. Another solution is to use a misting system. Some keepers spray the enclosure with a spray bottle and then cover parts of the enclosure to help keep the humidity levels up.

Hide Area

Hide areas are very important elements of good enclosures. Hide areas provide a sense of security to hatchlings and adults alike. They are necessary for a tortoise's emotional well-being.

A variety of items can make wonderful hide houses. Some choices are rounded cork bark, half logs, commercial reptile "caves", or even a shoe box with a hole cut in the side! The idea is to provide a dark, quiet retreat. The possibilities are endless. Flower pots turned on their sides, commercial shelters, or even hide houses made of wood are all acceptable choices. The hide area should be placed in the cooler, darker side of the enclosure. Damp sphagnum moss should be added under the hide area to keep the humidity up inside.

Water

Clean water should be available to your tortoise at all times. The water bowl must be large and shallow enough for the tortoise to easily climb in and out of. Make sure the water is not too deep for delicate hatchlings. Hatchling Redfoots should be placed in their water bowl or soaked twice a week. There are a variety of water bowls on the market that are suitable. A plastic coffee can lid makes a nice shallow water dish for hatchlings.

Decorating Your Enclosure

Enclosure decorations can add beauty and a more natural look to your tortoise's living area. Live non-toxic plants will add security and additional hiding spots for your tortoise. It's rewarding to make your

A Cherryhead Red-footed tortoise explores its enclosure. The cork bark cave provides a shelter at night.

enclosure as natural for your tortoise as possible. Be sure not to put obstacles too close to a heat lamp as you don't want the tortoise to flip over under the heat lamp. A well-planted or creatively decorated enclosure is both aesthetically pleasing and offers stimulation to the tortoise.

Planting Enclosures

Adding live non-toxic plants to your enclosure will add beauty and produce a more natural environment. In some cases, potted plants may be added that droop over the sides of the pot, offering additional hiding places. Be sure the plants are free from pesticides and herbicides. If your substrate is deep enough you may plant them directly in the enclosure. Make sure the soil they are in is free of the tiny white Styrofoam balls nurseries use to keep the soil loose. These are dangerous as hatchlings may ingest them and become impacted. Some keepers plant grass seed right inside the enclosure. This will offer an additional food source and encourage grazing behavior once your tortoise is outdoors. A hatchling's ability to recognize additional food sources such as grazing mediums when they are young will carry over to healthy eating habits as adults. Some keepers grow a variety of grazing mixes in cat litter pan type containers. Clippings are then taken off and offered to the tortoises.

Safety Tips

Clamp lamps with ceramic bases are imperative to prevent a fire. Also, ceramic heat emitters decrease the chance of a fire.

Make sure a lamp will handle the wattage of bulb you are using and that it is firmly secured to avoid falling.

* UVB lamps can be tested for output with a UVB tester.

In summary, indoor enclosures should be as large as possible for your space allotted. Tubs and enclosures are available both online and at specialty pet stores. The enclosure should be longer than it is wide to offer a temperature gradient that allows a tortoise to move from a warm area to a cooler area.

Proper lighting is essential to the health of your tortoises. Supplements and Vitamin D3 are needed to process calcium.

Humidity is important in the substrate to decrease the chances of dehydration and pyramiding.

A hide house should be placed in the cool darker side of the enclosure to offer security and a retreat away from heat and intense lighting.

Decorating your enclosure with live or fake plants will offer security and beauty.

Chapter FIVE: Outdoor Enclosures

This well-planned enclosure is secure from predators and also provides the tortoises living within access to fruit, leaves, and flowers.

Husbandry issues are one of the most important considerations in keeping Red-footed and Yellow-footed tortoises healthy. Their environment should replicate that of their native habitat as much as possible. Ideally, outdoor pens should be provided for the warmer months. The same considerations that apply to indoor enclosures are just as important when building an outdoor enclosure. The size of the enclosure, a clean water source, shade, hide areas, and security are all aspects of planning a suitable outdoor living habitat.

Enclosures for Small and Medium Tortoises

Even young tortoises benefit from sunlight but there are more considerations related to their safety. Young tortoises and hatchlings will overheat much faster and should be closely monitored in the sun. Shaded areas are essential to keep this from happening. Very young tortoises should not stay outside full time and should not be left unattended outside for the first year or two. Never put a glass enclosure outdoors. They heat up quickly and can have devastating effects on your tortoise.

Often a young tortoise will be very excited to be outdoors. They will be eager to explore their enclosure with wide eyes and increased activity levels. Be sure you don't have anything in the enclosure that can cause the tortoise to turn itself over. Tortoises may also flip themselves over by climbing walls and falling backwards. This is a particular concern in direct sunlight or in the heat of the day. You should check your tortoises frequently until they get used to their new surroundings. Flipping is also a concern when adding new animals (after quarantine) as they may flip each other over while becoming acquainted.

Predators

Predators such as birds can easily swoop down and steal a young tortoise. Other predators include raccoons, opossums, coyotes, and foxes. Any dogs should be kept away from tortoises both indoors and out. Most people cannot imagine their dog hurting anything however, every year hundreds of tortoises are killed or critically injured by dogs that have never hurt a fly. Be very careful your dog and any neighbor's dogs are kept away from tortoise enclosures. If you are

This outdoor enclosure is completely secure.

In areas where turtle predators such as raccoons, opossums, and foxes live, a secure wire mesh will need to be placed around turtle and tortoise enclosures.

going to take the youngsters outside it's very important to have them in a protected pen. Framing out a wooden top with hardware cloth is your best bet. You can even offer more shade by placing shade cloth or a piece of wood over the hardware cloth.

Sadly, another predator may be humans. Curious children have been known to steal tortoises. Adults knowing their value may steal them while you are away.

Other dangers outside, especially in the south, are Fire ants. Fire ants deliver a painful sting. Watch for Fire ant mounds. Fire ants can quickly kill smaller tortoises. They must not be allowed in your tortoise's enclosure. Here in Florida if we encounter the beginning of a Fire ant nest we cover the area with an overturned Rubbermaid tub. This will keep tortoises from walking directly over the mound. In the mornings, the Fire ants bring their eggs to the top of the nest to warm in the sun. That's when we pour large pots of boiling water over the top of the nest. Of course we then cover the area with the same Rubbermaid to prevent tortoises from being burned. Later, the nest is dug out and more water is poured if necessary. Never put poisons of any kind inside a tortoise's pen. Another trick that sometimes works is to spread dry grits around an ant mound. The worker ants will take the grits to the queen. She will eat them, drink water, and explode. Some keepers swear the smell of marigolds is an ant deterrent. We have not found them to do any good.

Size

A younger tortoise's enclosure should be at least 2' by 3' (61 cm x 91 cm) although if you make it larger they will have room to grow into it. You don't want to make it so large you will have difficulty finding the tortoise.

Substrate

The same substrate rules apply to outdoor pens. You want a substrate that will hold humidity. Peat moss mixed with organic top soil or mulch is a good option. You can place piles of moist sphagnum moss in their hide as well. We have multiple substrates in our outdoor enclosures. This offers the tortoise a choice of which they prefer. A grassy area is wonderful for grazing while a drier area of Florida sand may be preferred by some individuals. Their shaded areas are a mix of peat moss and organic top soil. Adding variety to their terrain makes the enclosure interesting and more natural. Unlevel ground may add visual interest as well as assist in breeding. (The adult tortoises may reach an area of unlevel ground that allows the male to more easily slip his tail under the female.)

* Don't forget to add a water bowl or water feature such as a shallow pool - one that your tortoise can easily climb in and out of. This must be kept clean at all times.

Larger Tortoise Enclosures

Your outdoor enclosure should be as large as possible. A minimum of 10' by 10' (3 m x 3 m) is recommended for an adult pair of Red-footed tortoise. As a rule of thumb you should provide a pen that is 10 times the length and 5 times the width of the tortoise. The larger you make your pen the better your ability to replicate the tortoise's

An outdoor Red-footed tortoise enclosure that offers live plants, access to water, shelters, and lots of natural sunlight.

natural environment. The sides of your pen should be from 16-18 inches (41-46 cm) high. While Redfoots and Yellowfoots are not generally diggers, they may work an area of fence not buried in the ground, particularly after a good rain. Sinking the walls of your pen at least 8 inches (20 cm) into the ground may keep predators out as well as prevent any attempted escapes.

Materials

Pens can be constructed from a wide range of materials such as pressure-treated plywood, concrete blocks, landscape timbers, sheet metal, PVC siding, and even chain link fencing. When using fencing it is a good idea to place a barrier around the bottom to avoid stress on your tortoise. If a tortoise can see through the enclosure walls it may climb or injure itself attempting to get out.

Planning Your Pen

When planning your pen, try to situate the pens so it receives southern exposure. Having sun in your pen for most of the day will give you more of a choice of where to add shaded areas. Whenever possible try to include non-toxic trees within your enclosure.

A Red-footed tortoise enjoying the water feature in its outdoor enclosure.

Water

These tortoises love to soak!

I cannot emphasize enough the importance of clean, accessible water. There are a variety of items that can be used for water bowls. Cement bird baths (taken off the stand) sunken into the ground work well.

Some keepers use planter saucers sunk into the ground. You can also use the flatter trash can lids, (new, of course) or even construct a shallow pond from concrete. It's a good idea to add a drain if building a concrete pond. This will make cleaning much easier. I use planter saucers in addition to a shallow pond made from a pond liner. This is very easy to clean by simply pulling the liner up, scrubbing it off, and replacing it. We have two liners so one can be bleached and dried in the sun while the other is in use.

A water area in which tortoises can climb in and soak is ideal. Place the water area in the shade to avoid water that gets too warm or blooms with algae. Yellow-footed tortoises may spend hours soaking themselves in a cool pond during the heat of the summer. Red-footed tortoises may do the same. Be sure the soaking area is shallow enough for them to climb in and out of easily. It's vital to keep the water clean. Water should be changed every day. Tortoises should not be allowed to drink water that has in it feces, mosquito larvae, and bacteria. I wouldn't ask my tortoise to drink any water I wouldn't drink myself.

Humidity

Keeping the humidity level high may be difficult in outdoor enclosures especially if you live in an area that is dry much of the year. Some keepers in areas of lower humidity utilize sprinklers or misters to keep the humidity levels up. Greenhouses are also used by some keepers, even in Florida, where the relative humidity is usually about 80%. Other ways to keep the humidity up in outdoor pens is to simply provide a humidity-holding substrate and hose down the tortoise enclosure on a regular basis. A humidity holding substrate such as mulch will help retain the moisture as well.

Planting Your Enclosure

A planted enclosure has many benefits. In addition to adding beauty, planting your enclosure can offer security, shade, and mental well-being for your tortoise. When planting your enclosure try to incorporate existing non-toxic trees and other plants. Plants such as Hibiscus, Banana palms, Mulberry, and Rose of Sharon can add beauty as well as provide food. This of course will depend on what will survive in your climate. To keep plants from being eaten completely, such as the Hibiscus, we bury the plant in the ground and then split the container it came in. The split container is then placed around the base of the plant to keep tortoises from devouring it before it even gets a chance to grow. Throughout the warmer months, flowers can be picked off and given to your tortoise as a treat.

Redfoots and Yellowfoots enjoy grazing just like other tortoises. Be sure any plants in your tortoise's reach are not toxic. Most herp societies and several Internet sites have large lists of edible as well as toxic plants. Keep in mind that plants from nurseries may have been sprayed with pesticides or herbicides. These chemicals can kill your tortoises.

Visual barriers

When planting your pen, try to create visual barriers. When keeping groups of tortoises this will offer security and alleviate stress for the females who may not want to be bothered by males in the mood to breed.

Security

It's your responsibility to keep your tortoise safe. When housing your tortoise outdoors you need to consider just how safe their pens are from predators such as raccoons, opossums, foxes, and even rats. Smaller tortoises left uncovered in open pens can fall prey to birds. Better safe than sorry! Always cover small enclosures with a hardware cloth, chicken wire, or another medium that protects them.

Larger pens can be protected with electrical wire. If you do decide to use an electric fence charger be sure they are allowed in your neighborhood if living in the city. They can be harmful to domestic animals as well as children. If you decide to use a plug-in electrical fence charger, it's easiest to use near an outlet. If no outlet is available, an insulated line can be dug three inches into the ground and run to the unit. Electrical fences are not 'set it and forget it' tools for protecting your tortoises. Routine checks should be made of the perimeter to make sure the wire is not touching the fence or a tree branch. This will cause the unit to short out and lose its effectiveness.

Solar-powered electric fence chargers run off the sun's energy. These are convenient because you won't have an electrical cord lying around.

Fully enclosed pens are another option to provide security.

Shade

Offering your tortoise proper shade is just as important as giving it access to the sun. Tortoises must be provided with the ability to cool

A plastic dog house and well-placed plants provide a secure resting area for captive tortoises.

off when they are too warm. This can be accomplished in several ways. Properly planted pens will have shaded areas the tortoise can retreat to. Also, shade cloth can be added to sections of the pen to shade entire areas.

Remember: Tortoises can overheat and die.

Hide Houses

Hide areas are essential to a tortoise's mental well-being. Hide areas will offer tortoises a sense of security, a retreat from other tortoises, and shelter from the elements.

Hide areas should be placed in existing shade if possible. A good insulated dog house such as an igloo works well. We use plastic dog house halves. Usually the section that sits lower to the ground is preferred. Ironically enough, when given a choice between a very large hide house such as a Rubbermaid bike shed or the dog house, our tortoises have always preferred the dog houses. Even when five different hide areas are offered, all six of our tortoises in this particular pen choose the house that is lowest to the ground. They also choose to crowd in together as opposed to having a more spacious retreat. According to the Vinkes (2008), burrows may be occupied by several tortoises at one time as they seek refuge from the heat or other elements. This may explain this behavior in captivity. I believe that while this 'crowding together' may seem like unusual behavior, it reminds us that Red and Yellow-footed tortoises are social animals.

In states that get thunderstorms and large amounts of rain you will need to study the areas of your pen that flood. In some cases, the tortoises may delight in soaking in the natural rain puddles, however they must not be forced to stay in them. They should have a choice. Hide houses should be placed on higher ground to keep them from flooding.

Hide houses can also be custom made of pressure-treated wood. Some keepers even add vinyl siding for a finished look. Insulated handmade hide houses can also keep the temperatures cooler for the tortoises in the heat of the summer.

Mixing Red-footed and Yellow-footed Tortoises Together

While the husbandry needs of both of these tortoises is similar, I do not recommend mixing these two species together in indoor or outdoor pens. A particular concern is the transmission of disease, some of which have no outward symptoms (See health chapter).

Supplemental heat

Red-footed and Yellow-footed tortoises do not hibernate. When the seasons start to change you must check your local weather forecast and plan accordingly. In some cases, hide houses can double as a source of supplemental heat. Redfoots and Yellowfoots should not be allowed in temperatures lower than 60-65° F (16-18° C). When the days are still warm but the nights begin to get chilly, heat sources such as a ceramic heat emitter or a pig blanket can be added.

Any heat source should be run through a thermostat for better control. Make sure any heat sources are placed at least 12 inches (30 cm) above the tortoise. If living in a cold climate the heated house should not be used as the sole enclosure. This is designed to keep the tortoise warm on chilly nights.

Do not lock tortoises in heated areas. Indoor enclosures will serve much better in states that are colder a larger portion of the year. In some cases, a large Rubbermaid tub may be used if you are simply housing the tortoise indoors overnight.

Winter Set ups

Note: When it is simply too cold for your tortoise to be outside for prolonged periods of time, other indoor accommodations must be provided. (see Indoor Enclosures)

We use a 20' by 20' (6 m x 6 m) insulated shed. We separate tortoises by species (never mix species) and offer them individual pens with the amenities they would have outdoors. Heat, water bowls, and hide houses help relieve the stress of being handled and brought indoors.

Other Heat Sources

Electrical heaters can be very dangerous. If you are going to use supplemental heat in a tortoise shed the safest heaters are radiator type heaters. They work by warming the oil inside to radiate heat from within the unit. There are no red hot coils that can easily catch on fire.

WARNING: Many tortoises have died as a result of a failed heat source going off at night. Make sure you have the right size fuses to prevent this from happening. Heating elements can cause a power overload and cause the power to fail, tripping breakers.

On occasion, in rural areas such as mine, I may experience power outages. I remedy this by keeping a generator and electrical cords close by, just in case.

Always keep a fire extinguisher near a shed used to keep tortoises warm. You can never be too safe. In case of power failure during a cold night you may want to get an alarm. These alarms can be programmed to emit a high-pitched siren if the temperature goes below or above the settings you program into it.

Summary

Tortoises are always happier outdoors. Outdoor enclosures should replicate their natural environment as closely as possible. Keep their

A large Red-footed tortoise explores its surroundings.

water easily accessible and clean. Offer choices of multiple hiding areas placed in existing shade. Hiding areas offer a retreat from the elements and a sense of security. Tortoises that have a retreat are less likely to become stressed. Planting your tortoise's enclosure with non-toxic plants, trees, and shrubs will offer additional shade, security, and an additional food source. Be sure to check your local weather forecasts to make sure your tortoise does not get too cold. Supplemental heat may be added or your tortoise may have to retreat to an indoor enclosure for the winter months. Address any security issues to keep your tortoise safe. Following these guidelines will allow you to enjoy your tortoise while it lives as naturally as possible for many years.

Chapter SIX: Feeding

Red-footed tortoises enjoying a diet of mixed vegetables and leafy greens.

In nature, Redfoots and Yellowfoots consume a diversified diet of high fiber leafy foliage in addition to some fruit, live prey, and carrion. Tortoises in nature are opportunistic. I can almost picture a tortoise wandering around in their natural range taking a few bites of several different plants before moving on to the next. If it tastes good to them, they eat it. In captivity any object introduced into their enclosure, whether indoors or out, is tested as a food source. I have introduced a colored feeding platter that was bitten by each and every tortoise in the enclosure. Once they realized this was not a new food item they simply walked away.

Feeding in Captivity

Many health problems in the Red-footed and Yellow-footed tortoise can be linked directly to an improper diet, being either from excesses (such as protein) or deficiencies such as vitamins and minerals. In captivity, we cannot offer the hundreds of different plants tortoises forage on in the wild. Therefore our goal is to provide a diet that is as variable as possible. It simply cannot be over stated, variety is the key to optimal health when caring for these tortoises in captivity.

Fresh leafy greens that are high in calcium and low in phosphorous are a good staple. A good feeding routine would be a variety of greens and vegetables for two days, adding fruit on the 3rd or 4th day. Favorite fruits are cantaloupe, mango, papaya, grapes, strawberries, and apricots. Redfoots love bananas but bananas should only be fed in moderation if at all. They can be addictive.

Food Addictions

Fruit in captivity should be limited to 1-2 times a week. Sugary fruits fed in high amounts are likely to become addictive, in addition to upsetting the digestive tract. Bananas are a good example of an addicting food. Tortoises becoming addicted to certain foods may refuse to eat anything else. This will make it very difficult to provide them with a proper diet that includes all the nutrients they need. Tortoises acquired already displaying signs of food addiction can be enticed to eat the right foods by offering the food they are addicted to in very small amounts mixed with the proper foods you would like them to be eating. Gradually decrease the addicted food until their diet has been corrected.

Fiber

Fiber is a very important part of your tortoise's diet. Fiber retains moisture and aids in the digestion of the foods your tortoise eats. In the wild, tortoises will eat dozens of various plants that have the fiber they need. Our attempts to replicate this in captivity are by offering a diverse diet of high fiber leafy greens and vegetables.

Here are some foods commonly enjoyed by the Red-footed tortoise. (Be sure all grocery store greens are thoroughly washed and free of pesticides.)

Romaine lettuce
Red leaf and green leaf lettuce
Chicory and Endive

Escarole
"Spring mix" (assortment of baby lettuces)
Collard greens (in moderation)
Dandelion greens
Turnip greens (in moderation)
Radicchio
Cucumber
Zucchini squash
Pumpkin
Chickweed
Mixed grasses, flowers, and clover
Zucchini
Carrots (on occasion)
Mushrooms
Bell pepper
Cooked or grated sweet potato (on rare occasions)

Protein

Protein should also be given, but in moderation. Most tortoises will eagerly feed on night crawlers, hard boiled eggs, meal worms,

An adult Red-footed tortoise eating a mouse.

chicken (cooked), and pre frozen pink mice. Some keepers may offer a high quality low fat cat food. Animal protein should be offered once a week, but no more than twice a week.

Protein is especially important for breeding age females. While Yellow-footed tortoises are also omnivores, they do not appear to be to the extent that Redfoots are. When coming upon carrion in their outdoor pen, the Redfoots fed voraciously upon a snake (also high in protein and calcium), while the Yellowfoots ignored even a dead mouse that was offered. It's important to note studies of the nutritional needs of tortoises, especially those concerned with protein are not an area well-documented.

We do know excess protein can contribute to pyramiding and a lack of protein can result in locomotion difficulties in the rear legs. We have seen the result of a lack of protein first hand while taking in rescued Redfoots. Often, the tortoise can not walk normally. Upon questioning of the owner about the diet, we often hear that the tortoise's diet was void of any animal protein. Within a few months of receiving a proper diet, the tortoise regained a normal and upright gait.

Feeding Fruit in Captivity

There is some debate as to the correct percentage of fruit the Red-footed tortoise consumes in nature. This of course is directly related to their geographical location and the availability of fruits in that region. In some areas, there may not be any fruit at all. According to Vinke and Vetter (2008). "The idea that Red and Yellow-footed tortoises eat lots of fruit, and even require it is still a widely held misconception."

While some authors recommend fruit as being as much as 70% of a Redfoot's diet we believe this percentage should be much lower. A good indicator there is too much fruit in the diet can be seen in the consistency of the tortoises' fecal matter. Feces should be well-formed as opposed to the runny mess created by a tortoise that has been fed too much fruit. The water and sugar in fruit can lead to increased levels of protozoans and can create an intestinal irritation. Yellow-footed tortoises do not seem to develop this problem as their

The male Red-footed tortoise (left) seems more interested in the female tortoises than this healthy, diverse salad.

needs for fruit are slightly higher. Keep an eye on that fecal matter!

Fruits enjoyed by the Red-footed and Yellow-footed tortoises include apples (no seeds), Opuntia cactus fruit, figs, apricots, plums, papaya, mango, pears, kiwi, strawberries, cantaloupe, tomato, blackberries, watermelon, and peaches.

Live Plants

The use of grazing items will enhance both the diet and the natural foraging behavior in your tortoise. Some plants enjoyed by Red-footed and Yellow-footed tortoises include Hibiscus (leaves and flowers), Hosta, Mulberry leaves, "Hens and Chicks", dandelion, chicory, spineless cactus, Beauty Berry, mixed grasses, and clover. Be very careful all plants are free of pesticides before allowing your tortoise to graze on them.

Edible Plants as Food for Tortoises

Latin name	Common name/s
Achillea millefolium	Yarrow
Agave sp.	Agave
Alcea Rosea	Hollychock
Aloe Vera	Aloe
Althea officinialis	Marsh Mallow
Amoracia rusticana	Horseraddish
Anthriscus sylvestris	Cow parsley
Bellis perennis	English Daisy
Buddleia spp.	Butterfly Bush
Calendula officinalis	Pot Marigold
Capsella bursa-pastoris	Shepard's purse
Cichorium intybus	Chicory
Cirsium arvense	Canadian Thistle; Californian Thistle
Cynodon dactylon	Bermuda Grass
Dahlia spec	Dahlia
Daucus carota	Wildcarrot
Echinacea purpurea	Purple cone flower
Eriocephalus africanus	Wild rosemary
Festuca arundinacea	Reed fescue
Festuca pratensis	Meadow fescue
Festuca rubra commutata	Chewings fescue
Ficus carica	Fig
Foeniclum vulgare	Fennel
Hemerocallis sp.	Day lillies
Hibiscus rosa-sinensis	Hibiscus
Ipomoea batatas	Sweet Potato
Lamium album	White Deadnettle

Lamium purpureum	Purple Deadnettle
Malva sylvestris	Hollyhock or mallow
Mesembryanthemaceae family	Ice Plants
Morus spec.	Mulberry
Nasturtium officinale	Watercress
Opuntia spec	Prickly Pear
Origanum vulgare	Oregano
Petunia hybrida	Petunia
Phleum pratense	Timothy
Plantago major	Common plantain
Poa pratensis	Kentucky bluegrass
Portulaca oleracea	Purslane
Raphanus stivus	Radish
Ribes nigrum	Black Currant
Rosa canina	Wild Rose
Rosa gallica	Domestic Rose
Rubus fruticosus	Blackberry
Rubus ideus	Raspberry
Salvia offinicialis	Garden sage
Salvia pratensis	Meadow sage
Schlumbergera bridgesii	Xmas Cactus
Stellaria media	Chickweed
Taraxacum offinicialis	Dandelion
Trifolium hybridum	Alsike clover
Trifolium incarnatum	Crimson clover
Trifolium repens	White clover
Tropaeolum majus	Nasturtium
Verbascum densiflorum	Mullien
Viola arvensis	Field pansy
Viola tricolor	Johnny jump-up
Vitis vinifera / Vitis labrusca	Grapes

* A huge thank you to Joe and Karen Heinen from **Carolina Pet Supply** (http://www.carolinapetsupply.com) for this list. It has been compiled from Joe and Karen's many years of keeping and breeding tortoises in the best conditions possible. Visit their webpages at http://redfoottortoise.com/edible_landscaping.htm

TOXIC PLANT LIST

Common Name	Botanical Name
Aconite (Monkhood, Wolfsbane)	*Aconitum* spp.
Anemone (Windflower)	*Anemone* spp.
Anthurium	*Anthurium* spp.
Atamasco lily	*Zephyranthes* spp.
Autumn crocus	*Colchicum autumnale*
Azalea	*Azalea* spp.
Baneberry	*Actaea* spp.
Bloodroot	*Sanguinaria canadensis*
Boxwood	*Buxus* spp.
Burning bush	*Euonymus* spp
Buttercup	*Ranunculus* spp.
Butterfly weed	*Asclepias* spp.
Caladium	*Caladium* spp.
Calla Lily	*Calla palustris*
Castor bean	*Ricinus communis*
Cherry laurel	*Prunus caroliniana*
Christmas rose	*Helleborus niger*
Clematis	*Clematis* spp.
Daffodil	*Narcissus* spp.
Delphinium (larkspur)	*Delphinium* spp.
Dumbcane	*Dieffenbachia* spp.
Elephant ears	*Colocasia antiquorum*
Four o'clock	*Mirabills jalapa*
Foxglove	*Digitalis purpurea*
Giant elephant ear	*Alocasia* spp.

Gloriosa lily	*Glonosa superba*
Heavenly bamboo (nandina)	*Nandinaa domestica*
Honeysuckle	*Lonicera* sp.
Horse chestnut (Ohio buckeye)	*Aesculus* spp.
Horse nettle	*Solanum* spp.
Hyacinth	*Hyacinthus orientalis*
Hydrangea	*Hydrangea* spp.
Iris	*Iris* spp.
Ivy (English ivy)	*Hedera helix*
Jack-in-the-pulpit	*Arisaemia triphyllum*
Jessamine (Jasmine)	*Cestrum* spp.
Jetbead (Jetberry)	*Rhodotypos tetrapetala*
Jonquil	*Narcissus* spp.
Lantana	*Lantana camara*
Lily	*Lilium atamasco*
Lily of the valley	*Convallaria majalis*
Mistletoe	*Phoradendron* spp.
Morning glory	*Ipomoea violacea*
Oleander	*Nerium oleander*
Periwinkle (Myrtle, Vinca)	*Vinca* spp.
Philodendron	*Philodendron* spp.
Potato	*Solanum tuberosum*
Privet	*Ligustrum* spp.
Rhododendron	*Rhododendron* spp.
Schefflera	*Schefflera* spp.
Sweet pea	*Lathyrus* spp.
Wisteria	*Wisteria* spp.
Yellow allamanda	*Allamanda cathartica*

* For a complete list of toxic plants, visit Joe Hienen's webpages at http://www.redfoottortoise.com/toxic_plants.htm

Many other herpetological clubs also offer extensive lists of edible plants. Be sure that all plants are free of pesticides and herbicides.

Feeding Multiple Tortoises

I feed my tortoises a staple diet of high-fiber greens. I try to use a mixture of 4-6 different types of greens and 2-3 different types of vegetables. I add the leaves and flowers of Hibiscus plants right onto their platters. Try to arrange their food on the plate so each tortoise has a variety directly in front of them. On occasion there will be a tortoise that sits directly in the food plate or walks around, picking out their favorites. If food is placed around the edges of the platter it is easily accessible to all.

This is also an important consideration when feeding hatchlings, to assure equal access to the food. Some tortoises may have to be offered their own plate to make sure they are not eating too much of one thing. I offer the platters every 3rd day. In the days inbetween, my tortoises walk around foraging on natural graze that has been provided in their outdoor enclosure. I offer fruit once a week, again making sure there are at least three or four different kinds.

Preventing Impactions

When feeding your tortoise, try to keep their food off the ground. Rubbermaid lids, restaurant trays, or stepping stones make wonderful platters. This will decrease the chance of your tortoise ingesting substrate or harmful bedding. Remove all food when your tortoise has finished eating. This will decrease flies, ants, or other pests.

* Remember never use commercial foods as a staple. If you're going to use them at all, use them sparingly. Some commercial foods claim they are made to be the sole food source. This is simply not true. The percentage of fiber in most commercial diets is very close to the percentage of protein. Red-footed and Yellow-footed tortoises need more fiber and less protein. As research into dietary needs of Redfoots and Yellowfoots progresses, so do the attempts to make a pelleted food that replicates their nutritional needs. For instance, Zoo Med has come out with an all-natural tortoise food that has a great variety of nutrients compressed into pellet form.

Many foods compressed into pellets contain undesirable ingredients such as grain, wheat, or rice. Heinen notes negative effects of a

Squash, melon, a variety of greens, and even flowers can provide the perfect Red-footed tortoise meal.

grain-based diet such as leeching of the bone, the binding of calcium and other minerals, and a negative impact on bone growth (Heinen, 2007, 2009).

Foods to Avoid

Foods high in oxalate acid should be avoided. Oxalates can contribute to problems in renal and bone development. Some examples of plants with oxalates are spinach, chard, rhubarb, beet greens, cabbage, kale, and broccoli. Many of these items are also very high in oxalic acid. Oxalic acid binds with nutrients, including calcium, and makes them inaccessible to the body. While some foods have properties that are good for the tortoise they may also be high in oxalate acid. The pros and cons should be carefully weighed. This is another reason why variety is so important.

Calcium

Calcium is essential for healthy bone development. Calcium is one of the most important minerals in a tortoise's diet and is especially important for hatchlings and for egg-laying females. Lack of calcium can lead to many health problems including MBD (Metabolic Bone Disease), soft shell, bone deformities, and in severe cases, death.

Sources of Calcium

The best source of a calcium supplement to use is a phosphorus-free calcium carbonate. This type of calcium may be purchased in a powder form. You can also buy it in a tablet form and crush it yourself into a fine powder. Sprinkle it over your tortoises' food several times a week. In the growth phase of your younger tortoises or for egg-laying females, use it at least three times a week. This form of calcium is very absorbable.

Cuttlefish Bone

Cuttlefish bone, or Cuttlebone, is sold in pet stores in the bird supply area. It can be used as a secondary source of calcium. This calcium source is not as absorbable as calcium carbonate (Highfield, 1996). Be sure to cut off the rough backing.

Calcium can only be metabolized by your tortoise with Vitamin D3 present.

Vitamin D3

Vitamin D3 allows the body to absorb calcium, and allows the body to maintain a proper balance of calcium and phosphorus. When phosphorus levels in the blood are too high the body takes calcium from the bones to bind with phosphorus and facilitate its removal from the bloodstream.

Tortoises that spend most of their time outdoors (several hours a day of direct sunlight) do not need Vitamin D3. They will produce their own by absorbing UV rays from the sun.

Captive tortoises not exposed to natural sunlight or high quality UVB emissions will need a supplement mixture of calcium with D3 added.

Other Supplementation

It is nearly impossible to replicate the natural diet of Red-footed tortoises and Yellow-footed tortoises. To make sure your tortoise is getting all the nutrition they need to stay healthy we recommend using a broad-spectrum mineral supplement. Rep-Cal® makes a balanced supplement called Herptivit™. We use this supplement once a week.

The use of grazing items will enhance both the variability in diet and the natural foraging behavior in your tortoise. There are numerous websites that sell carefully prepared natural supplements and seeds to grow your own grazing forage.

Some of these include:

www.Carolina PetSupply.com
www.Turtlecafe.com
www.Turtlestuff.com
www.reptigreens.com

Water

Water is essential to the healthy life of your tortoise. Clean water should be provided at all times. Many health problems can be linked to dehydration. Be sure to clean your tortoise's water every day to avoid ingestion of fecal matter, mosquito larvae, or bacteria.

Summing it Up

As noted, variety is the key in a captive tortoise's diet. Red-footed and Yellow-footed tortoises need a staple of leafy greens high in fiber in addition to moderate levels of fruit and protein.

Never feed the same food every day. Mix it up!

Do not overfeed the wrong foods or use commercial diets as a staple. However varied your diet is, I still recommend the use of a mineral supplement once a week.

Calcium is vital to bone and shell health. Proper use of calcium will stop many problems before they get out of hand, such as MBD and growth deformities. Calcium cannot be absorbed without Vitamin D3. Be sure you have the correct exposure to natural sun, UVB emitters, or a calcium supplement with Vitamin D3.

Feeding your tortoise is one of the best parts of being a keeper. It's fun to watch them enjoy a proper diet that will keep them healthy. Remember, variety is the key!

Chapter SEVEN: Health

A pair of healthy, alert, active Red-footed tortoises - the goal of every keeper.

General Health

Red-footed and Yellow-footed tortoises are hardy if their habitat is maintained properly. A humid substrate, proper temperatures, lighting, fresh clean water, and a correct diet are all key elements to preventing most health issues.

Sometimes tortoises get sick even if they are receiving proper care. In some cases, illnesses are not displayed in the form of a symptom until the disease or condition has progressed significantly. For this reason it is very important you learn the routine and behaviors of your tortoise. If even slight changes occur you will know immediately and be able to act. Make sure any changes in behavior are not temperature related. Other changes in behavior could be linked to a female needing to nest. Some contributing factors that predispose your tortoise to illness are stress, parasites, an improper diet, and dehydration.

Stress

Stress can contribute to a variety of health problems. Tortoises under stress can have compromised immune systems making them more susceptible to pathogens. Improper husbandry is a major factor that can cause stress to tortoises in captivity. To eliminate stress make sure your tortoise has a large enough enclosure to get away from other tortoises if they desire. Additional hiding places may be necessary to offer a greater sense of security. Proper substrates, diet, and correct heating and lighting all contribute to the emotional well-being of your tortoise. In some cases, males may have to be separated from each other during breeding season and the female they may be pursuing. Enclosures that are crowded with aggressive cage mates can also make a tortoise vulnerable to stress. Make sure their enclosures are large enough. Egg-laying females may also experience stress if not provided with a suitable nesting area or if they are competing for suitable areas with other females.

Parasites

Many health problems can be caused by untreated heavy parasite loads. Parasites are part of a tortoise's natural system in nature. Elevated levels of parasites can cause serious medical problems. In the wild a tortoise moves around at will, occupying a much larger area than provided in captivity. Tortoises living in captivity and defecating in a compacted area allows the probability of continued and increased infestation. This is particularly noteworthy in dealing with wild-caught tortoises. The presence of parasites can be detrimental to health and needs to be dealt with immediately.

Fresh imports of wild-caught tortoises have been found to have infestations of the flagellate, *Hexamita parva*, *Entamoeba invadens*, and nematodes.

Symptoms of worms are a strong smelling urine, loose pungent or bloody stools, excessive drinking, anorexia, lethargy, and in some cases visible worms in the feces. Tortoise stools should be firm and full of fiber, not runny. Your tortoise should be taken to the veterinarian for a fecal examination. A fecal exam is important to identify the culprit and to use the correct de worming agent. Treatments for parasites are carried out according to the parasite and the life cycle of the parasite.

A series of fecal exams should be done until they come up clean.

There are many types of worms and parasites such as protozoans and helminths. Protozoans are single-celled organisms such as flagellates and amoebas. Helminths include flatworms, tape worms, and roundworms.

Some common wormers used on tortoises are Fenbendazole, Metronidazole, Praziquantel, and Iodoquinol.

Panacur® (Fenbendazole) is used for the elimination of many parasitic worms.

Flagyl® (Metronidazole) treats amoebic parasites, flagellates, and gram negative organisms.

Droncit® (Praziquantel) treats cestodes (tapeworms) and trematodes (flatworms).

Yodoxin® (Iodoquinol) treats infections caused by protozoa and intenstinal infections caused by amoebas.

Administration of Worming Medication

On occasion, it may work to put medication on your tortoise's food. However, if the tortoise is not eating, the dose may have to be given via a feeding tube. This is the recommended method to assure an accurate dosage and delivery.

Some de-worming agents can be hard on your tortoise's system, killing beneficial bacteria as well as the parasites. There are products on the market that will help restore the positive fauna to your tortoise's digestive system. We use a product called Bene-bac™. A routine trip to your veterinarian for an inexpensive fecal is recommended once a year or if there are symptoms. Never give medications without consulting a qualified veterinarian.

IVERMECTIN WARNING!

Ivermectin is a very well-known anti-parasitic medication used by veterinarians to combat nematodes and even ticks and lice. It is relatively safe when used on mammals in the proper doses, but it should never be used on a turtle or a tortoise. It crosses the blood-brain barrier and can result in paralysis and death in turtles and tortoises.

External parasites

External parasites include ticks and mites.

Ticks may occasionally find their way to your tortoise, especially if your tortoise lives outdoors. This is also a concern in dealing with fresh imports. Ticks can drain your tortoise of energy and blood. Ticks can also transmit disease. Ticks can sometimes go unnoticed if they are up high on the rear legs or close to where the skin hits the shell. Gently remove ticks with tweezers. If you twist the ticks counter clockwise as you pull, mouth parts are less likely to stay in the animal. You can also cover the tick with Vaseline. This will

Even though most Red-footed tortoises are captive-hatched or farm-raised, any new tortoise should be checked for ticks and other parasites when it arrives in your home.

suffocate the tick, causing it to back out. Wipe down the area where the tick was embedded with an antiseptic wipe.

Mites may be very hard to see because of their small size. You may notice them as tiny white specks in the water dish, particularly in an indoor enclosure. The easiest way to get rid of mites is brushing them off with diluted Betadine and then changing the substrate.

Maggots are fly larvae that may be deposited in an open wound. If this occurs, they will have to be manually removed one by one. The wound can be flushed with Betadine or Hydrogen peroxide to make sure no maggots remain.

Dehydration

Fresh, clean drinking water must be available and accessible at all times. If you don't think your tortoise is drinking enough soak them in shallow water several times a week. Some tortoises will not drink from standing water. If your tortoises will not drink from a container try running a garden hose next to them. We have had good luck with this method.

Signs of dehydration are decreased skin elasticity, skin that looks dry, decreased urine output, sunken eyes, and weight loss.

Normal urate waste should be clear mucus. Tortoises secrete waste as uric acid. This requires them to absorb large amounts of water. If dehydration occurs uric acid becomes insoluble. The bladder will reabsorb the urinary water causing the urates to crystallize and eventually become bladder stones. Chronic dehydration and excessive protein can lead to gout. Gout occurs when the level of uric acid in the blood is more than the kidneys can remove. Uric acid that crystallizes in the joints is called articular gout. Uric acid that crystallizes in other organs is called visceral gout. It's very easy to prevent this from happening by simply providing a clean water source. Symptoms of gout are enlarged or painful joints and stiffness. Gout is diagnosed by radiographs.

Some other health problems affecting tortoises include respiratory problems, mouth rot, injuries, and septicemia.

This Yellow-footed tortoise arrived at a veterinary clinic with pneumonia and a severe parasitic infestation.

Respiratory Problems

Symptoms of respiratory problems are wheezing, rubbing of the eyes or nose with the front legs, a discharge from the nares (nostrils) or mouth, and, in extreme cases, open mouth breathing with an extended neck. A very weak tortoise may extend his head and allow it to drop lifelessly to the ground. Tortoises may sit for hours or days with their legs out to get maximum air into their lungs.

Respiratory problems can affect the upper respiratory tract (URTD). This affects the sinus or nasal area.

Respiratory problems can affect the lower area (trachea or lungs) too. This is referred to as lower respiratory disease (LRDT). Because tortoises do not have a diaphragm, they are unable to cough to expel mucus and secretions. Retained mucus can cause a simple respiratory infection to progress to pneumonia (Frye, 1991).

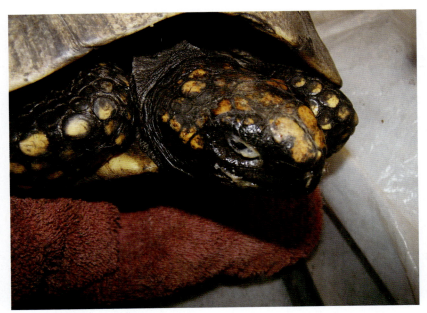

This very sick Yellow-footed tortoise has sunken eyes and a thick discharge from the eyes, nose, and mouth.

Respiratory problems can occur with a weakened immune system proliferated from a poor diet, improper temperatures, parasites, stress, or bacteria. They can also be secondary to other medical conditions. Respiratory illness should be diagnosed by a veterinarian through cytology or culture and sensitivity testing. A culture should be taken from the inside of the tortoise's mouth or the fluid dripping from the nares (nostrils). The culture will be sent to a lab. The lab report will show what, if any, bacteria are present and what the bacteria is sensitive to in the way of an antibiotic treatment. The veterinarian will then determine the best choice of antibiotic therapy. In some cases, the veterinarian may prescribe a broad spectrum antibiotic while waiting for test results.

In some cases, respiratory problems will be diagnosed by radiographs. Tortoises should be kept in a clean, simple enclosure during treatment. Proper hydration during antibiotic therapy is crucial.

Nebulizers are often effective in the treatment of lower respiratory diseases. Using a nebulizer will put medication directly into the lungs and speed up recovery.

Some respiratory issues can be directly related to husbandry issues. For Redfoot tortoises, make sure the substrate remains moist. Substrate that dries out may get dusty and cause irritation to the eyes or lungs.

Fungal Infection and Shell Rot

Improper husbandry practices that lead to dirty conditions can suppress a tortoise's immune system. These conditions create an opportunity for bacteria and fungus to grow. Infections of the shell can be bacterial "wet" rot, which is also called Ulcerative Shell Disease or fungal "dry" rot. Infections can also be a combination of both. Shell issues need to be dealt with immediately as they can lead to deadly systemic infections.

Fungal infections on the shell may appear as white powdery, pitted, or flaking patches. Left untreated, fungal infections will eat away at the keratin of the shell. Excessive moisture or dead matter in a tortoise's enclosure provide the perfect environment for fungus to grow. Fungal infections are fairly easy to remove.

Shell rot in a Red-footed tortoise.

Shell rot or Septic Cutaneous Ulcerative Disease (SCUD) is typically seen as pitting or ulcers of the shell. When the shell acquires an abrasion, is scratched, injured, or punctured, there is an opportunistic route for fungus or bacteria to grow. Any abrasion can lead to infection below the keratin.

Mild shell rot or fungus can be treated by using a diluted povidone-iodine solution (Betadine) or a diluted chlorhexidine (Nolvasan) solution (1:10 diluted with water). The area should be scrubbed gently with a soft bristled tooth brush.

Deep, foul-smelling or bleeding rot will need immediate veterinary attention. The veterinarian may culture the area, remove necrotic tissue, or prescribe antibiotics or antibiotic creams.

You can prevent shell rot or fungus with clean husbandry practices. Never leave rotting food within an enclosure. Check your tortoise's plastron often to make sure it is not coated in fecal matter or rotting food. Give the entire shell an inspection frequently and keep habitats clean!

Safety Tip

Wash your hands! Turtles and tortoises can carry salmonella. Hand washing with an antibacterial soap will keep you from getting sick. Always wash your hands before moving from species to species to avoid cross-contamination. Always keep turtle water away from dishes and areas in which food is prepared for you or your family.

Mouth Rot (Stomatitis)

Mouth rot is a term used to describe mouth infections. Infections can be viral, fungal, or bacterial in nature. Mouth rot has the appearance of a bumpy white "cheesy" raised area in the mouth and tongue area. Tortoises affected by mouth rot may also display redness inside the mouth and a discharge. A swab should be taken for a culture. This condition requires immediate veterinary intervention as advanced cases can go into the bone. Conditions that attribute to mouth rot are poor husbandry inadequate temperatures, or poor jaw alignment caused by an overgrown beak.

Herpes Virus

Herpes virus is a life-threatening disease affecting tortoises. A herpes virus infection can lead to respiratory distress, nasal and oral discharge, oral lesions, mouth rot, edema, bacterial and fungal infections, and death. The herpes virus is contagious through contact with body fluids. Redfoots and Yellowfoots have been reported to be infected with the herpes virus. Herpes is diagnosed through a culture or a blood test.

Whenever a wild-caught animal is purchased, an oral examination should take place to check for mouth lesions. If a tortoise is found to have these lesions, be extremely diligent in monitoring the tortoise. It is best to keep this animal by itself and in an indoor enclosure.

Be very careful when adding new adults to your group. Follow strict quarantine practices. Herpes virus can wipe out entire collections. Sometimes the infected animals may not show any symptoms yet still carry the deadly virus and spread it to others. Yet another reason why you should acquire disease-free captive-bred specimens.

Lesions

Occasionally a tortoise may get a cut or scratch. The area should be cleaned and rinsed with diluted Betadine or Nolvasan (9:1) solution. Watch the area carefully for any signs of swelling or infection. Keep the tortoise on a clean towel indoors until healing is evident. Tortoises with injuries of this nature run the risk of flies and a maggot infestation. Deep wounds that may require stitches will have to be dealt with by your veterinarian. Wounds left untreated run the risk of progressing to septicemia.

Deep wounds such as dog bites require immediate veterinary attention. If the wounds are not life-threatening, secondary infections that can occur certainly are.

Septicemia

Septicemia is a generalized systemic infection usually caused by a gram-negative bacteria that enters the body through a cut or a sore.

This is a life-threatening condition that requires immediate veterinary care.

Symptoms of Septicemia

1. **Lethargy** is a symptom of septicemia that is often overlooked. This is why it's so important to observe your tortoise for changes in behavior. A tortoise that is usually active but suddenly stays in one spot or acts unusually tired warrants further investigation.

2. **Red flush** or pinkish flush to the shell or soft skin may manifest in severe cases. It's important to point out that a tortoise can still be septic without this symptom.

Splotchy redness may develop on the tongue or inside of the mouth.

3. **Excessive drinking** . A tortoise that can't seem to get enough to drink or drinks so much that they vomit is another sign.

Diagnosis: Septicemia is diagnosed through a blood test.

Some other conditions that can lead to health problems are MBD, overheating, impactions, and poisoning.

Metabolic Bone Disease (MBD)

Metabolic Bone Disease occurs when there is inadequate calcium, Vitamin D, or the absence of UVB light in a tortoise's environment. MBD will cause softening of the shell and malformation of the shell and bones. Hatchlings and egg-laying females are particularly affected. Hatchlings, because of their rapid growth have higher calcium needs. The lack of enough calcium will leave them with soft, pliable shells and deformities such as pyramiding. In severe cases the bony tissue will thicken in the jaws and limbs. When there is inadequate calcium in the bloodstream the parathyroid gland attempts to compensate for the deficiency by moving calcium from the bone to the bloodstream. Left untreated, MBD is a life-threatening condition. This condition is entirely preventable with good dietary management.

To prevent MBD, reptile keepers must provide the animals in their care with access to direct sunlight or UVB-emitting lamps, proper diet and supplementation, and the correct temperatures.

For tortoises living outdoors, calcium with no phosphorus and without Vitamin D3 should be provided twice a week in the form of a powder lightly sprinkled on their salads and/or addition of cuttle bone to the enclosure.

Calcium for hatchlings or tortoises living indoors should be phosphorus-free. The use of calcium with Vitamin D3 is debatable among some keepers and breeders. Some breeders feel Vitamin D3 should be given in the form of a good UVB light while others feel hatchlings in the wild spend most of their time hiding so Vitamin D3 is not necessary during the first six months of a tortoise's life. Our hatchlings are treated just like our adults in this aspect. The general belief is to use calcium with Vitamin D3 when the tortoise is housed indoors. Miner-all I can be used once a week to supply trace minerals that may be lacking in a tortoise's diet.

DO NOT over supplement! Over supplementation can lead to dehydration and creation of dangerous bladder stones.

Over-heating

Hatchlings are particularly prone to the dangers of over-heating. Never place a glass terrarium in the sun. Hatchlings that do not have a retreat from extreme temperatures can rapidly over-heat. Adult males in combat during mating season may flip their opponents onto their backs. If the upended tortoise does not right himself and is left upside-down in the sun he may over-heat as well. Symptoms of over-heating are a heavy saliva discharge from the mouth and the tortoise being very warm to the touch. Slowly cool the tortoise down by running their body under tepid water and gradually decreasing the water to cold. Be careful of the face. Seek the advice of a qualified veterinarian. To prevent over-heating, make sure the tortoise has a shaded retreat. Also, inspect to be sure cage decorations are not too close to a heat lamp.

Poisoning

Poisoning can occur from the use of toxic garden chemicals such as pesticides, weed killers, or rat poison. Never use these chemicals near your tortoise's enclosure. If poisoning occurs, every effort should be made to identify the toxin. Seek veterinary treatment immediately. Poisoning may also occur from the ingestion of toxic plants. Be sure to check lists of toxic plants before introducing them into or near your tortoise's enclosure. Toxic tree leaves hanging over the tortoise enclosure can be harmful. Plants that are edible may also be dangerous if recently sprayed with pesticides.

Impactions and Colic

Most impactions can be completely avoided. At feeding time be sure to place your tortoise's food on a plate or platter. Never place food directly on the ground. Substrate may accidently be ingested. For larger tortoises, Rubbermaid lids work well. For smaller tortoises you can use smaller Tupperware lids or plastic plates.

Colic occurs when intestinal gas reaches large quantities. This dietary problem can be avoided by limiting sugary fruits and foods that are high in carbs. Untreated impactions can cause septicemia. Impactions and colic are diagnosed by a radiograph (x-ray).

Vitamin A Deficiency

Symptoms of Vitamin A deficiency include inflammation of the eyes, nasal discharge, and dry sloughing skin. Many times Vitamin A deficiencies are misdiagnosed as the symptoms are very similar to other illnesses. The veterinarian may extensively evaluate the diet or take tests to see if a Vitamin A deficiency is truly the cause of illness. A change in diet is the safest way to correct any deficiencies.

Vitamin A Overdose

Vitamin A overdose can have devestating side effects, often after injections of Vitamin A by a veterinarian. The side effects of Vitamin A overdose are similar to those seen in Vitamin A deficien-

This is an older Red-footed tortoise (note the smooth shell) but it is obviously healthy and alert. These tortoises can live for many years in captivity when their needs are met properly.

cies. Skin sloughing may leave raw skin with the potential for secondary bacterial infections.

These are just a few conditions to affect the health of your tortoise. There are many other scenarios not mentioned here. Symptoms requiring immediate medical attention include:

1. Loss of appetite
2. Lethargy
3. Excessive drinking
4. Sunken or swollen eyes
5. Discharge from the nose or mouth
6. Foul smelling, runny, or bloody fecal matter
7. A red flush to the skin or shell
8. A white or pale tongue
9. Edema (swelling)
10. Difficulty walking

If your tortoise is displaying one or more of these symptoms it's time for a trip to a qualified reptile veterinarian. Some veterinarians claim to work on tortoises but actually have no experience with them. Make sure the veterinarian you use is qualified (with references).

It is not advisable to self-treat your tortoise or take advice from the internet (a lot of it is wrong). Diagnosis should only be obtained from a qualified veterinarian who can physically examine your tortoise. The time to have a qualified reptile veterinarian is before you need them!

Search for a veterinarian with reptile experience in your area at the Association of Reptile and Amphibian Veterinarians (ARAV) website at http://www.arav.org

In summary, many health issues with your tortoise can be prevented. Proper heat, proper diet, and constant hydration are essential to overall health. Knowing your tortoise's routine will allow you to question any activity that deviates from what is normal for your tortoise. Have the phone number to a qualified veterinarian handy so you don't have to search for one during an emergency.

Chapter EIGHT: Breeding, Eggs, and Incubation

Male Red-footed tortoises can be very persistent and if a female becomes stressed from his constant advances, she should be moved to another enclosure for a break.

The ultimate goal of many keepers is the ability to maintain adults that are healthy enough to breed. Before you decide to breed your Red-footed or Yellow-footed tortoises, you should consider what you will do with the hatchlings. Every effort should be made to make sure they end up in knowledgeable hands, and with keepers where they can spend a good deal of time in outdoor enclosures.

Proper conditions such as general health and diet are factors that contribute to a tortoise's ability to breed and lay eggs. Make sure your tortoises are healthy and fed a proper diet before allowing them to breed. Breeding tortoises that are not healthy can have devastating consequences. For instance, tortoises that have been fed an improper diet may have slow or no egg production. If they are able to reproduce the yolk sacs of their hatchlings may not contain enough nutrients for the embryo to develop. This may manifest in partially developed tortoises that die in the egg (Heinen, 2009). We have experienced this unfortunate event with rescue tortoises that were fed an improper diet and were gravid upon arrival.

In the wild, Redfoots generally mate at the start of the rainy season. They will breed year round in captivity. In nature, the breeding season may be different in each geographical location. In some areas of South America, the breeding season may last 2-3 months. For some, it may be from July to September, while others are from November to February. The seasons of the Northern hemisphere (USA) are opposite of the seasons in the Southern hemisphere (South America). Our summer is their winter. However, Redfoots and Yellowfoots live mostly north of the equator in areas that don't really experience a "winter".

Sexing RED-FOOTED TORTOISES

Identifying male and female tortoises is fairly easy if the specimens are full grown or nearly full grown. The males have a deeply indented plastron. Sometimes this concave indentation is extreme

Plastrons of an adult male (left) and adult female (right). Note the differences in the shapes of the anal notches and concave plastron of the male.

and sometimes it is more subtle. Females have little or no plastron indentation but not nearly as pronounced as the males. The shell of male Redfoots is slightly constricted in the center, giving them the appearance of having a waist line when viewed from above. While this is a good indication that your tortoise is a male, in tortoises from some areas this slimming is slight or nonexistent. Male Cherry heads lack the waist line.

The tails of male Red-footed tortoise are considerably larger and longer than those of the female.

The anal notch is located on the plastron just anterior to the tail. The anal notch of a male is wider, less pointed, and has a thickened edge. This configuration allows for maximum tail movement for mating with females.

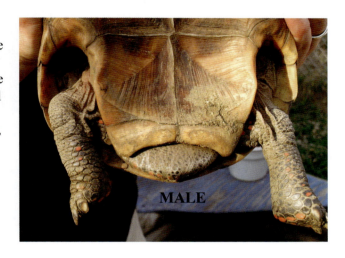
MALE

The female's anal notch is more narrow and angular. Some male Red-footed tortoises are more

FEMALE

The deeply concave plastron of a mature adult male Red-footed tortoise.

brightly colored than the females. The author has noticed that even at the time of hatching, the brighter colored babies generally turn out to be males.

Courtship

There are several cues and behaviors that keep Red-footed tortoises from hybridizing with other tortoises, especially Yellow-footed tortoises. According to Pritchard and Trebbau (1984), the bright color of the head and legs of Red-footed tortoises is most prominent in areas in which they occur with or near Yellow-footed tortoises. This may explain why the Yellowfoots and Redfoots do not hybridize.

In addition, male Redfoots display specific head movements during courtship and breeding behavior. These specific movements may also prevent the Redfoot from breeding with other tortoise species.

During courtship, male Redfoot tortoises usually stand on the side of the female tortoise. He may circle her repeatedly with an extended neck. He will move his head in rapid jolts to the side and back to the middle. While many other species of tortoise display frontal head bobs, Red-footed tortoises have a distinct series of jerking motions. The male will also make a series of clucking noises that rise and fall in pitch. He will follow the female and attempt to mount. Copulation is often highly vocal and can be heard from quite far away.

Yellow-footed tortoises are more likely to breed in the rainy season. They can be aggressive and vocal breeders. While the Redfoot's head movements are a jerking sideways motion Yellow-footed tortoises display a constant swoop from side to side when pursuing a female.

Males may chase or ram females they intend to breed. Our observations indicate that the ramming stops when the female remains still. Often, the male will circle the female, occasionally sniffing her cloaca.

During copulation, the male will vocalize with a series of grunts and clucking.

The male stores sperm and the female produces eggs. The eggs reach development before the shell is formed when the eggs are

Copulation in a pair of healthy Red-footed tortoises. Photo by David Lee / Tortoise Reserve.

A female Red-footed tortoise depositing her eggs. Photo by Marty La Prees.

fertilized. Fertile eggs do not require the tortoises to mate each time. Many females can store sperm for up to five years. So, even if no male is around a female can still lay fertile eggs. It's very important to make sure your female has enough calcium during breeding season.

Rival males sometimes attempt to flip over any competitor in their enclosures. They may display the series of jerking motions to each other, however females do not usually display this behavior.

Red-footed tortoises can start producing eggs at about 8 inches (20 cm). Often first clutches will be small and infertile. As the tortoise grows closer to their adult size, the eggs will be larger and have a much better chance of being fertile.

Nesting

A female Red-footed tortoise that is ready to nest will often pace back and forth aimlessly looking for just the right nesting site. This behavior may be observed days before the actual nesting will take

Red-footed tortoise eggs incubating in vermiculite and then covered with damp sphagnum moss.

place. Often female tortoises lay eggs in the same vicinity year after year. Sometimes nests are partially dug and abandoned. This is not uncommon. When she finds the best spot, females often go into a "laying trance", obtaining a far off look in their eyes.

Generally in the late afternoon, and even more likely after a gentle rain, nest digging begins as the female tortoise slowly pushes dirt off to the sides. using one back leg at a time. She will rotate her legs, pushing dirt away as her egg chamber is slowly and meticulously formed. An area directly above her tail is deepened as each leg takes a turn excavating. The nest depth will depend on the individual tortoise. Some are surprisingly shallow while others can be 5-6 inches deep. Generally the nest depth will be deeper than her legs can reach, causing her body to shift slightly to either side as she gets the legs as deep as possible into the chamber. She will then collapse the ledges, causing the chamber to become wider. It's amazing how their instincts tell them how large to make the nest. When the nest is dug to her satisfaction, she will point her tail downward and begin to lay the eggs, sometimes pushing up slightly on her back legs. Eggs will slide down a mucus sleeve which decreases their speed to the bottom of the chamber. After the eggs are laid she will gracefully position the eggs with her back feet before she begins to fill in the nest. Once she fills the nest with rotating legs, she will pack the dirt flat on the top of the nest. This process usually begins in the late afternoon. The process can take from 1-3 hours. This process is usually not completed until well after dark. Never disturb a female until she has finished laying the clutch of eggs and begins to bury the eggs.

A female Red-footed tortoise will lay 3-5 eggs though more have been reported. Nests may go unnoticed as they do a great job of blending them into the environment. A female can lay two to three clutches per year.

Yellow-footed tortoise females typically lay from 4 to 12 eggs. The larger clutch size is more typical of the Amazon Basin Yellow-footed tortoises that grow much larger.

They may produce as many as four clutches during mating season at intervals of 3-4 weeks. Yellow-footed tortoise females may dig a shallow nest or simply lay their eggs in piles of leaves, under the base of a plant, or in a moist area in their enclosure.

It's crucial to the health of an egg-laying female to make sure they are getting enough calcium.

Egg-laying Indoors

Redfoot females can lay clutches of eggs in indoor enclosures without any problems. If your tortoise is displaying signs of pacing or restlessness she may be ready to nest. A veterinary appointment may be necessary to confirm the presence of eggs.

A large Rubbermaid bin can serve as a laying area for tortoises that must be indoors due to inclement weather. Make sure you have between 10-12 inches (25-31 cm) of a substrate that holds its shape such as a 50/50 mix of top soil and damp sand. Tortoises that do not have an adequate spot to lay eggs may experience egg binding.

Egg binding / Dystocia

Locomotion difficulties or difficulty walking can be a sign of egg binding. Egg binding occurs when the female tortoise retains eggs within her body and is unable to lay them. One cause of egg binding is the inability of the eggs to pass through the oviduct and cloaca. The eggs may be too large to pass through the pelvic canal, may be misshapen, or may be blocked by an obstruction. Other causes of egg binding may be inadequate nesting areas or improper nutrition.

Retained eggs put painful pressure on internal organs and must be removed. Watch your tortoise carefully if attempts at nesting occur over a week. If your tortoise stops eating or appears weak it's time for a trip to the veterinarian. Egg binding is a serious medical condition that requires immediate veterinary attention. Again, symptoms can be difficulty walking or lethargy. Egg binding is diagnosed through a radiograph. If a radiograph, or x-ray, determines the eggs can be safely laid by induction of oxytocin (causes contractions) your veterinarian may need to intervene. Like antibiotics, oxytocin should never be given blindly. This is for your veterinarian to determine. Tortoises that require oxytocin to lay their eggs should be handled properly before the injection. The tortoise should be well-hydrated. A tortoise given oxytocin that is not adequately hydrated runs the risk of the eggs being broken inside of her. This is a life-threatening incident that causes a major infection.

Another concern is calcium. Some veterinarians administer calcium 12-24 hours before using oxytocin. Calcium is absorbed into the body very quickly. Egg shells that are too thin may break. If oxytocin does not work or if the eggs are not in a position to be laid, surgery may be necessary. This is usually only in extreme cases.

Incubation

Natural Incubation

Eggs may be left in the ground to hatch. Eggs left in the ground may remain viable even over the winter. When during the season they were laid has no impact on their hatchability. Eggs left in the ground will hatch in the summer when the rain softens the soil, allowing the babies to dig out of the ground. This method is not recommended in some of the southern states where there are Fire ants. Fire ants are attracted to the yolk and mucus covering hatchlings and can quickly kill them. While I may occasionally miss a nest, there are simply too many predators in my area that are attracted to the eggs. These include moles, Pine voles, shrews, and raccoons. I choose to keep eggs safely indoors and incubate them there.

So, outdoor nests must also be protected from other predators. If you know where the nest is located, carefully cover it with a wire cage that is strongly attached to the ground. This cage will keep out any predators that may dig up the nest.

Artificial incubation supply list

An incubator, an incubation medium, a container large enough to hold your eggs, a hole punch for making air holes in the lid, A hydrometer, a thermometer, and a spray bottle for misting the eggs and inside the incubator to raise the humidity level.

Artificial incubation

Have your incubator ready! This means the incubator should have a stabilized temperature. It's advisable to have an incubator stabilized several days in advance of placing the eggs inside. We just leave ours plugged in during breeding season so they are ready to go.

There is a variety of incubators on the market from the $50.00 range to the more elaborate $400.00 models. We use Hovabators sold

An inexpensive incubator that can be used to incubate tortoise eggs.

by the Randall Burkey Company. They manufacture an incubator especially for use with reptiles.

Temperatures

Red-footed tortoise eggs are temperature sex-dependent. Incubation temperatures above 88° F (31° C) will produce females while temperatures below 82° F (28° C) will produce males. The ideal temperature if both sexes are desired is between 84-86° F (29-30° C). Higher temperatures can result in shell deformities.

Humidity

The humidity in the incubator should be about 80%. This can be measured with a hydrometer available at most pet stores or on-line.

The incubator should be opened at least twice a week to allow fresh oxygen to reach the eggs. If the humidity needs to be raised, placing a small cup of water inside the incubator helps. If proper humidity levels are not met there is a chance the baby tortoise will not be able to break out of the egg. We also put pieces of damp sphagnum moss over the top of the eggs.

Be sure to put the sensor from the temperature and humidity gauge inside the container that contains the eggs for an accurate reading. Mist the eggs as needed. For me, this is about once every 1-2 weeks. Eggs kept too moist run the risk of absorbing too much moisture and cracking open too early.

Incubation Substrates

You will need a Tupperware container or tub large enough to hold all the eggs, and the lid that comes with it. You can use Tupperware, Glad ware, or any other plastic container that will fit into your incubator. Make sure your container is not so tall that it hits the heating element of the incubator.

Fill the container with vermiculite moistened with water in equal weights. The substrate should be moist not soggy. The substrate should hold its form when lightly squeezed together, and not be dripping wet. It is always better to have the incubation substrate a little bit too dry than too wet. In wet substrate, the eggs will absorb too much moisture and the developing embryo will die.

There are other mediums on the market such as perlite and a fairly new substrate called Hatch Rite™. Hatch Rite™ works very well and is already premixed with water. A mixture of half perlite and half vermiculite with the same weight of water added can also be used.

Red-footed tortoise clutches usually ranges from 3-12 eggs. Mine generally lay 4-6. The size of the eggs depends on the size of the female laying them. Eggs generally weigh from 35-50 grams.

Removing the Eggs from the Nest

Carefully remove the eggs from the nest and place them just as they were found into the Tupperware container about an inch deep in the substrate. We generally gather the eggs before the female finishes burying them. Be sure not to stress her and if you are going to do this approach her slowly. Occasionally eggs will break as she is depositing them into the nest hole. Even if you carefully catch the eggs as she lays them, always allow her to finish covering the hole. Never turn the eggs after 24 hours of them being laid. This will usually kill the developing embryo. With a soft lead pencil, carefully put an X and a date on the top of the egg. If an egg is accidentally moved, you will always know where the "top" is.

Once you have the entire clutch, place the lid on the Tupperware container and place it in the incubator. Make sure to poke some holes in the lid for ventilation. Do not incubate eggs in air tight containers. Eggs incubated in air tight containers run the risk of accumulating carbon dioxide levels. This can cause the death of premature hatchlings. These gases can be absorbed through the shell just as moisture is absorbed. Make sure you write down the date the eggs were laid! Fertile eggs will hatch in 129 to 175 days at a temperature of 86° F (30° C).

For Yellowfoots, incubation times are variable from 130-150 days. Yellowfoot hatchlings have a serrated edge around their shells. Redfoot hatchlings do not have this characteristic.

Incubation Problems

Sometimes an egg will start to split much earlier than the anticipated hatching time. If this happens try taping the split with a small piece of Tegederm. This has worked for me on many occasions. The egg has hatched later with its siblings.

Note: Higher incubation temperatures - above 89° F (32° C) - can result in shell deformities.

The humidity in the incubator should be about 80%. This can be measured with a hydrometer available at most pet stores. The incubator should be opened at least twice a week to allow fresh oxygen to reach the eggs. If the humidity needs to come up placing a small cup of water inside the incubator helps.

Be sure to put your temperature and humidity gauge inside the container that contains the eggs for an accurate reading.

Hatching Your Own Redfoots

The hatching process may take several days. Never pull a baby tortoise from its egg or do anything to interfere with the hatching process.

It is very exciting to watch a baby tortoise emerge from the egg, especially for the first time. For me, the joy of watching tortoises hatch is just as exciting each time.

When the due date for the Redfoot hatchlings gets closer, it is helpful to mist the eggs more often. Before the eggs start to hatch you may see tiny cracks in the eggs. This is where the hatchling is using its

A Red-footed tortoise hatches in the warmth of its incubation container.

caruncle, or egg tooth, to break through the egg. This is called pipping.

The hatching process may take several days.

Occasionally a hatchling's yolk sac may be large or ruptured. In this case you want to apply a small amount of diluted Betadine (9 parts water to 1 part Betadine) to the area and rinse well.

I make a donut with a moist paper towel or a coffee filter. Place the moistened paper towel in a thoroughly cleaned container such as a deli cup or an earthworm container. I place the baby in the center. This will take the pressure off of the yolk sac.

Cover the hatchling with another small moist paper towel and return it to the incubator. By returning the tortoise to the incubator, you are putting it into a dark, warm, and safe environment. In the darkness, it will be less inclined to try to move around and injure itself.

The Future

A juvenile Yellow-footed tortoise explores its outdoor enclosure. Photo by Bill Love.

The Red-footed and Yellow-footed tortoises, with their bright inquisitive eyes and attractive coloration, have captured the hearts of many tortoise keepers. It's no wonder these beautiful and personable tortoises are rapidly becoming a favorite species to keep in captivity.

Red-footed and Yellow-footed tortoises are easy to breed in captivity if their diet and husbandry is correct. The future of the Red-footed tortoise in captivity is bright. Though the Yellow-footed tortoise is not bred in the large numbers that Redfoots are, they are increasing in availability. There is a wealth of information pertaining to their care in books, care sheets, and on the Internet.

Unfortunately, Red-footed and Yellow-footed tortoises struggle for survival in their native countries. Their future in many areas is grim. Tortoise populations are under extreme pressure and are rapidly decreasing. They are caught for food and eaten in large numbers. Dogs are trained to hunt tortoises, and areas are burned to force them out of hiding. Considered a food source over much of their range, they are inhumanely slaughtered. Many countries in South

Cherry head Red-footed tortoise. Photo by Jake Kirkland.

America are predominantly Catholic and turtles are considered fish by the Pope. Thus, during Lent and fish days, the native people not only eat tortoises on a regular basis, but have learned they can sell them to Christians by standing along the highways with live tortoises. The enforcement varies from country to country and administration to administration. These tortoises bring top dollar in food markets in major cities. Many households have captive tortoise that they may keep for years, but eat the biggest and heaviest for Lent. It is a tradition and they must have their tortoise on the table. It's expected as much as a Thanksgiving turkey (Lee, D., pers. com.). In some parts of South America, Red-footed and Yellow-footed tortoises can no longer be found even though they were once abundant. They are exported by the thousands for the pet trade and their habitat is being destroyed and altered. Even conservation measures are subject to loop holes that threaten their numbers with exploitation.

There is no reason to buy wild-caught Red-footed and Yellow-footed tortoises when hatchlings are so readily available from tortoise breeders. Buying captive-bred tortoises will allow you to raise a wonderful, healthy baby and take some pressure off the wild populations. Also, the pet trade animals are often those that were not sold for Lent and so the animals are additionally dehydrated and stressed, and tend to not fare well. There is no telling what they have been through before they arrived in your home, how long they have gone without food and water, or if they will ever acclimate to life in captivity.

I hope this book will help you enjoy your Red-footed and Yellow-footed tortoise as much as I have mine. With tips you will receive about proper diet, supplements, setting up indoor and outdoor enclosures, and health information, a tortoise can be an interesting part of your family for years to come.

* When you are ready for a more indepth look at Redfoots and Yellowfoots, I hope you will purchase my book **REDFOOTS & YELLOWFOOTS: *The Natural History, Captive Care, and Breeding of Chelonoidis carbonaria and Chelonoidis denticulata*** from LIVING ART publishing (isbn 0-9787556-3-4).

PHOTO GALLERY

A beautiful captive-hatched Red-footed tortoise whose parents originated from Colombia. Photo by Bill Love.

Head detail of a beautiful Cherry head Red-footed tortoise. Photo by Sam Floyd.

A dark, melanistic Red-footed tortoise. Photo by Marc Cantos.

A beautiful albino Red-footed tortoise. Photo courtesy of Fred Gaal.

SUGGESTED READING

Alderton, David. 1988. Turtles & Tortoises of the World. New York & Oxford (Facts on File).

Bartlett, R. D. and P. Bartlett. 1996. Turtles and Tortoises: A Complete Pet Owner's Manual. Barron's Educational Series, Inc. Hauppauge, N.Y.

Ebenhack, A. 2009. Redfoots and Yellowfoots: The Natural History, Captive Care, and Breeding of *Chelonoidis carbonaria* and *Chelonoidis denticulata*. Living Art publishing. Ada, OK.

Gurley, R. 2006. Sulcatas in Captivity (With Notes on Other Popular Tortoises). ECO publishing. Lansing, MI.

Highfield, A. C. 2000. The Tortoise and Turtle Feeding Manual. Carapace Press. UK.

Highfield, A. C. 1996. The Practical Encyclopedia of Keeping and Breeding Tortoises and Freshwater Turtles. Carapace Press. UK.

Klingenberg, R. 1993. Understanding Reptile Parasites. Advanced Vivarium Systems. Lakeside, CA.

Lowe, P. 1997. Redfoot tortoises: South American treasure. Reptile & Amphibian Magazine. 1997(Mar./Apr.):36-43.

Metrailler, S. 1997. *Geochelone carbonaria*. Reptilia. 3(9):53-55.
Paull, R. C. 1999. Tortoises of the World: The Great Red-foot Tortoise *Testudo carbonaria*. Green Nature Books, Homestead, FL.

Pingleton, M. 2001. Practical Care and Maintenance of The Redfoot Tortoise (*Geochelone carbonaria*) in Captivity. Carapace Press.

Pritchard, P. C. H. 1979. Encyclopedia Of Turtles. T.F.H. Publications, Inc. Neptune, NJ.

Pritchard, P. C. H. and P. Trebbau. 1984. The Turtles of Venezuela. Society for the Study of Amphibians and Reptiles, Oxford, Ohio.

Vosjoli, P. de. 1996. The General Care and Maintenance of Popular Tortoises. Advanced Vivariums Systems. Lakeside, CA.

Resources

Places to Buy Supplies Online

Doctors Foster & Smith
www.Drsfostersmith.com

Carolina Pet supply
www.Carolinapetsupply.com

LLL Reptile
www.lllreptile.com

Places to Buy Seeds and Supplements

Carolina Pet supply
www.Carolinapetsupply.com

Turtle Cafe
www.Turtlecafe.com

Turtle Stuff
www.Turtlestuff.com

Adoption/ Rescue Services

Turtle Rescue USA
www.Turtlerescueusa.com

Turtle and Tortoise Preservation Group
www.ttpg.org

Mid-Atlantic Turtle and Tortoise Society
www.matts-turtles.org

Turtle Homes
www.turtlehomes.org

The Turtle Center
www.turtlecenter.org

Turtle Rescue of Long Island
www.turtlerescues.com

California Turtle and Tortoise Club
www.tortoise.org

Conservation

The Tortoise Reserve
www.tortoisereserve.org

Turtle and Tortoise Preservation Group
www.ttpg.org

The Tortoise Trust
www.tortoisetrust.org

The Turtle Survival Alliance
www.turtlesurvival.org

Locating a Reptile Veterinarian

www.arav.org

www.repticzone.com/articles/reptileveterinarians.htm

www.anapsid.org/vets

www.herpvetconnection.com

About the Author

Amanda Ebenhack has been keeping and breeding Red-footed tortoises for 10 years. She is a permitted wildlife rehabilitator in Florida, specializing in tortoises. Together with her veterinarian, Dr. Orlando Diaz of Lake Howell Animal Clinic, they rescue, rehabilitate, and release between 100 to 500 turtles and tortoises each year.

Amanda is a member of the Turtle and Tortoise Preservation Group, a board member of the Asian Turtle Consortium, a board member and director of adoptions for Turtle Homes Rescue, and president of the Central Florida Wildlife Center.

In 2009, Amanda was honored with the Barb Bonner Memorial Award. The Bonner Award is presented each year by the Asian Turtle Consortium at the National Reptile Breeders Expo and is given in recognition of expertise in long-term husbandry and captive breeding of turtles, especially Asian species.